How ~~to be~~
Zoomly®
at work

THE ESSENTIAL HANDBOOK
FOR THRIVING AT WORK

Dawn Sillett

How to be Zoomly at work

First published in 2014 by

Panoma Press
48 St Vincent Drive, St Albans, Herts, AL1 5SJ, UK
info@panomapress.com
www.panomapress.com

Book layout by Neil Coe

Printed on acid-free paper from managed forests.

ISBN **978-1-909623-58-3**

The right of Dawn Sillett to be identified as the author of this work has been asserted in accordance with sections 77 and 78 of the Copyright Designs and Patents Act 1988.

A CIP catalogue record for this book is available from the British Library.

This book is available online and in bookstores.

Dedication

To Chris

Testimonials

"This incredibly comprehensive, jargon free volume ought to be a permanent aide memoire for every manager"

**Patrick Mills,
Director of Professional Development, IPA**

"Throughout my career, Dawn has coached me to take the right steps at times of change at work. Particularly useful are her practical exercises and visualisations, all laid out in the book. "How to be Zoomly at Work" is almost like having Dawn on tap in an easy-to-read form. Worth referring to whenever you run up against hurdles, dips in self-confidence or just require the clarity to make the right decisions. Her approach to personal and professional growth at work is refreshingly simple, and positive."

**Laura Jordan Bambach,
Creative Partner at Mr President and
President, D&AD.**

Foreword

What does being 'Zoomly at work' mean?

Zoomly is the name of my company, which provides training and coaching to help people boost performance and accelerate their career progress. We're really focused on what we do well and work hard to deliver great results. Zoomly is about being focused and effective, so I'm guessing you're considering this book because that's what you want to be. Which is good, because that's the aim of this book.

I've been training and coaching professional creative people for around fifteen years, and have lost count of the number of times someone has come up to me at the end of a training workshop and said, "Can I just ask…?" and posed a question about something important to them. When I was a novice trainer I thought, "Weird… why didn't they ask that in the session?" Of course I was missing the entire point. They didn't want to ask their question in the workshop because they were wary of looking foolish, or seeming way adrift of the rest of the group, or of simply discussing their situation with someone on the same payroll. Over time I have learned to cherish these questions, because not only do they give me the chance to help someone, but chances are the person asking it was not alone in having that question. So now I think hard about the questions people ask me during and after our training workshops; they are a true reflection of what's going on for our course participants. People's questions provide priceless insights that help us better serve them. And what about the others who were in the room, who may also have had the same question racing round their head? Well, that's why I've written this book.

Please get in touch with any comments, feedback or questions about this book. dawn@zoomly.co.uk

How to use this book

Part I is all about you. Where are you now, and how did you get here? Where are you going? Where do you want to be? This section of the book aims to help you get completely clear on your career so far, and where you want to go in the future. To get the best from Part 1, I suggest you work through the exercises in order. Some are quick and simple; others ask you to dig deeper.

Part II is all about the people skills you need to navigate office life and succeed. In other words, how to be Zoomly at work. Having completed the exercises in Part 1, you can decide which areas in Part 2 are the top priorities for you. So you can zoom in on the chapters you most urgently want to work on, whether that's how to prioritise, delegate or give feedback.

How to be Zoomly at work is the final part, where you get ready to step up and apply what you've learned.

CONTENTS

How to be Zoomly at work

INTRODUCTION

You don't have to be a bitch or bastard to get promoted

Let's get this straight from the start: nice people do succeed! Really, they do. I can think of plenty, many of whom I've had the pleasure to work for, and with, and the privilege to have work for me. Think of the respected leaders in your field of work, your industry, sector, profession, and I bet you'll come up with some really great people who not only have a head for business, they have a heart and soul too.

Do you have to be tough?

You may be thinking, "I see lots of tough people get promoted". OK, that may well be true. So let's just deal with the tough thing first. What's 'tough' about? Are they decisive? Are they focused? Are they ambitious? Well, aren't you?

Or is 'tough' about how they do things? By yelling at people, bullying and table thumping, for example? My early experience of life in advertising agencies exposed me to plenty of this. I'll never forget the creative director who, when I walked into his office with my manager, addressed me and said, "Why the hell have you brought him?", or the senior director who was fond of throwing furniture. These days, thankfully, there's a lot less of that old school behaviour about. Indeed, the more extreme forms of throwing one's weight around probably fall outside the law now. If there's a moral in here, I think it's about choosing our role models with great care.

In some organisations, toughness is a requirement of the role: negotiating contracts with clients and suppliers, for example. Toughness may also be the word we use to describe the way in which someone has A Plan and executes The Plan, although they might use another word, such as determination, focus or persistence. We may perceive people who are aware of organisational politics and skillful at working with them as being 'tough cookies', yet they could describe themselves as simply 'smart'. They know how things work round the place, and the right levers to pull to achieve their aims.

Why do some people get promoted early?

People who get promoted early may have specialist knowledge or superb skills in a particular area, but they have something more that marks them out. I think a vital ingredient is how effectively they are able to work with other people. Over many years, it's been my observation that people who get promoted more quickly than others get the hang of some important points, fast. Here's what we can learn from them:

1. Know your strengths – and your weaknesses. You will get heaps of help throughout this book, especially in Chapters 1 and 2.

2. Bring out the best in others. Many an expert or specialist has had their promotion plans held up because of a need to 'boost your people skills'. If that's you, help is at hand throughout this book.

3. Develop office antennae. Identify significant stakeholders – the people with organisational clout and interest in your area of the business. Observe and learn how they prefer to get things done, and what they prioritise. This can help sharpen your commercial savvy; for example, how your employer makes (and loses) money. Focus on where you can make a difference. More on this in Chapter 9.

4. Communicate clearly, in different media. That means speaking clearly, writing clear emails, presenting clearly and being crystal-clear on the phone. More on this in Chapter 4.

5. Have A Plan. Carry it out. Stick with this book for help on both.

Take the real you to work

Here's the caveat to what I think it takes to stand out for the right reasons: none of it works if you're a fake. Trying to adopt a persona that just isn't you will make you miserable, is exhausting and won't work, or at least not for long.

Authenticity is essential. We humans are pretty good at spotting a fake. Be honest about where you're from and don't try to hide it. If you have worked your way up from humble origins, that's an important part of who you are. Ditto if you have had a more comfortable life so far: don't affect a downgrade just to try to fit in. That's what the next chapter is about – who are you, and how did you get to here?

PART I:

ALL ABOUT YOU

CHAPTER 1
HOW DID YOU GET TO HERE?

CHAPTER 2
WHERE ARE YOU NOW?

CHAPTER 3
WHERE YOU DO WANT TO BE?

CHAPTER 1

HOW DID YOU GET TO HERE?

When we're working hard, playing hard and generally being busy, time slips by and we often operate on default. The idea now is for you to stop, think and notice what you may have been taking for granted. It took me many years, a psychology degree, and extensive professional and personal development to get to grips with understanding my strengths and weaknesses. It need not take you that long. It's my aim to help you speed up that process in three steps:

- Success stories
- Obstacles and overcoming them
- How you got to here.

Gather your evidence

So this is a project – call it 'Project ME' – to set you on your way to achieving your potential. We're going to start with an inventory – a stock-take if you like – to get clear on how you got to here. You're going to be doing some research – about yourself. Treat this as a serious exercise and you will get valuable viewpoints and heart-warming insights into your potential. You're going to need some time to do the activities and tasks that follow. Some can be done in under half an hour, others will take longer – it depends on how easily you can write about yourself. Your evidence will come from multiple sources; that way it's a rounded view of you. Keep a notebook, build up your evidence in a folder, type it up on your laptop – however you do it, be sure to record every element you gather. For now, please just complete each task as you go: we'll review them all later.

"Can I just ask...
...does it matter if I don't have much experience?"

It depends on how you define 'experience': narrowly as in 'I've done X (e.g. presentations) in a paid job, from (date) until (date)', or broadly, as in 'I've gained valuable experience of X (e.g. presentations) in my gap year when I (e.g. taught schoolchildren); at university/college when I (e.g. took part in debates), and outside work when I (e.g. made a speech at a friend's wedding)'. If you go for a broader definition, chances are you'll be able to come up with examples of experience. This can be a useful exercise, and not just when you're job hunting; we often under-estimate the value of experience gained beyond work, yet it can be exactly what a potential employer wants to hear – and it's a positive boost to our self-esteem.

---

1. List your success stories

Do this exercise quickly to get started. Get pen and paper, tablet or laptop, and methodically list all your successes. All of them. Now's the time to really blow your own trumpet. Think of your school, college, university, sports, a community or club you joined, friends and family, hobbies, home, purely personal stuff such as health and fitness, and of course work. Stuck? Here are 10 possibilities to get your thinking started:

- Getting a badge for map reading
- Representing my school in the swimming team
- Getting into university
- Getting my first job
- Buying my first flat
- Passing my driving test
- Getting promoted at work
- Helping a relative with their C.V.
- Learning a foreign language
- Making a speech at a friend's wedding.

Keep going – you have lots of success stories to tell. Don't edit yourself – "oh, that really wasn't such a big deal" – get all your successes down, big and small. Come back and add to your list later.

2. Take credit for obstacles you have overcome

This activity may relate back to your success stories and is worth doing somewhere quiet. You might need to dig deep emotionally and you will need to be honest with yourself. We can brush aside the obstacles we have overcome in order to get to here and now. So think of the obstacles you have faced, what you did to overcome them, and the results you have achieved. You may have needed to learn a language, deal with family opposition, or recover from injury.

Obstacles	What I did	Results achieved

3. Chart how you got to here

Create a map of your journey so far: where you have lived, important events, significant changes, milestones, all the way to the job you have now. I've seen people create these maps quite quickly; others take time assembling and embellishing it. You choose. You can create a small drawing, make a collage, or buy lining paper from a décor shop and chart your journey horizontally over time. You might draw symbols for certain events or emotions. Use coloured pens, photos and cuttings from magazines. Put it on a wall at home and look at it for a few days, then add to it. However you visualise your journey so far is up to you, so long as you can see, at a glance, the route from its beginning to here and now.

Summary: how did you get to here?

1. Looking back is something we often neglect in the context of our personal and professional development.

2. Reflecting on our past is an essential part of learning who we are, and how we got to here.

3. If we just act without reflection, we risk repeating mistakes.

4. It's all too easy to overlook our individual success stories. Some of us are more hard-wired than others to dwell on failures. So it's essential to remind ourselves of what we have achieved so far.

5. Looking back at the obstacles we have overcome a) provides essential insights and b) reminds us that we can prevail.

You're going to look at all this information soon, but not just yet. Some people find these exercises and reflections tiring; others find them stimulating and energising. If you're feeling weary right now, take a break. Otherwise keep going to the next chapter.

Resources

If you have enjoyed the activities in this chapter, you may enjoy *Manage Yourself, Manage Your Life: Vital NLP techniques for personal well-being and professional success* by Ian McDermott and Ian Shircore. Whilst based on Neuro-Linguistic Programming (NLP), the exercises are very accessible to non-NLP-ers. Available on Amazon.

CHAPTER 2

WHERE ARE YOU NOW?

So you've got lots of ideas about how you got to here. Now you're going to add more information to your project, from a wider range of sources. This will help you get a clear picture of where you are right now. We're going to look at two key sources of information: assessments and people. There are two activities for you to try:

- Strengths assessment
- Interviews

About assessments

There are heaps of different kinds of assessments out there, from wild and wacky to those used by FTSE 100 companies on a regular basis. I'll give you a brief rundown of different assessments, including some you can access for low or no cost as part of your project.

Skills and capability assessments: Competency and capability assessments are generally used at the recruitment stage, and again when large organisations are looking to identify promotion prospects. These tend to be tests with scores (some organisations have a minimum pass mark), so need to be relevant to the role. Apply for a job at a blue chip company and the chances are you'll be asked to complete some of these tests online before you get to the interview stage. Some of Zoomly's corporate clients insist all job applicants pass Maths and English tests before going any further in the process: no mental arithmetic, no job. Also in this group of assessments are tools that can test your decision-making and critical reasoning capabilities, and of course your IQ. If you have any assessment results, add them to your evidence. If you want to have a go at this type of test, check out the resources section at the end of the chapter and add the results to your project.

Psychometric assessments: Psychometric assessments, or 'personality tests' to use the vernacular term (and inaccurate: you can't fail a personality test!), can also be used at the recruitment stage, although some are more appropriate for this than others. I think they are really valuable when people want to develop, get out of their comfort zones, raise self-awareness – and of course when you're pushing for promotion. You get a clear picture of your default settings, habits and preferences, and insights into why some of the stuff you experience happens. For more on these tools, check out the resources.

"Can I just ask...
...can I do a personality test?"

I often get asked if I've heard of or used certain psychometric tools and assessments, and whether they are any good. Some are more popular than others. Some are more robust than others. Some are older; some are newer. Some are the preferred tool for a particular organisation. I always recommend people check the test out, not only on the tool's own website, but also via The British Psychological Society, which has a Psychological Testing Centre guide for the public http://www.psychtesting.org.uk/ptc/roles$/the-public.cfm

360-degree feedback: This is when people complete online questionnaires or interviews about how they experience working with you. These people may be your boss, department head, peer from another department, people you manage, or clients and suppliers. Some organisations select who will provide the input and others ask the recipient to choose. In some cases the feedback is anonymous and in others it's attributed. You may get your 360-degree feedback landing in your inbox in the form of a report, or via a 1:1 discussion with a colleague or coach. By now I hope you're getting the idea that how these things are handled can vary enormously.

This kind of assessment can be pretty hard to argue with. Whilst some people may dispute the theory and provenance of psychometrics, what other people have to say about you is just that. It's their opinion, and if you disagree with it, you at least have to accept that they're entitled to it. That may not make it any easier to digest: way back when I first had this kind of assessment there were elements of it that felt like a slap in the face. But when I re-read the comments, which were from more than one person, I began to realise that they were right. There were things I had to improve upon – and thankfully there were some positives too. Got a 360? Add it to your project.

Strengths assessments: A more recent addition to the tools out there is strengths assessments. These do pretty much what you might guess: you complete a questionnaire and get back a report detailing your top strengths. There are versions where others contribute too. This approach has sprung up from the positive psychology movement, and is gaining ground. Whilst strengths assessments have a sound theoretical base, they are more user-friendly than some other tools and tend to use jargon-free language. I'm a fan of this approach, with one big proviso: sure, we all need to identify and use our strengths, but please let's call it like it is when it comes to our weaknesses – and deal with them. There are some low- or no-cost questionnaires you can access easily online, and that's what I suggest you can do right now: complete one of the strengths assessments listed in the resources and carefully study your profile report. Allow between 20 and 40 minutes to complete the assessment. Remember to add it to your project file. When you've done that come back and complete the next stage.

Interviews – just ask people: Now you'll need to take notes, or audio recordings, as you ask people who know you for their views. Aim for a cross-section from different aspects of your life, and start with those you find easiest to approach. That way, you'll get started and gain momentum quickly, rather than put this part off because it seems too hard; it really isn't – once you get started. You could get heaps of priceless information over just one weekend.

What to ask?

"What would you say are my top three qualities?" can be a good start. You're after positive input here, and people are generally only too pleased to provide it. And if you want to add a further question, try; "what one piece of advice do you have for me?" That ought to give you enough to get your teeth into, but if your research respondents offer more, consider it a bonus and note it all down.

How to ask?

You could, of course, simply post the questions on your social media pages, but I wouldn't recommend it for two reasons. First, you don't have to put yourself out there to the same extent you will when you pick up the phone or ask people face to face, and that is one of the key aims of doing this exercise. It takes courage to ask, so this will help you build your bravery muscles. Second, when you ask people for their input more directly, person to person, you will get much clearer and more honest responses from them. By all means use social media to make contact and arrange to meet/talk on the phone/Skype. What will you say to start the conversation? How about being honest and telling them you're doing a research exercise as part of a management development project that will help you progress in your career?

Who to ask?

People who know you and who you can trust. People with no agenda – so that rules out current colleagues. Friends old and new. Friends from childhood can be great fun, as can friends from school or university. Families are great respondents: those who remember you as a kid and those to whom you're a great big grown up. Members of clubs and community groups are also good: book clubs, gym or running clubs, alumni associations. Ex-colleagues, both peers and managers, can be really good to contact, but as mentioned above, leave current colleagues to one side for now.

By the way, be ready for your interviewees to ask you to reciprocate and give them your input on their top three qualities and one piece of advice! You might want to have these points prepared as a courtesy before you talk to people. However, take the temperature: they may not want your input, or maybe not right now.

Here's a chart to help you capture that information, or use as a template.

Interviewee name	My top three qualities	One piece of advice for me

Examine the evidence

Now you've completed your self-assessment and interviews. Add them to your work from Chapter 1 – your success stories, obstacles overcome and map of how you got to here. By all means gather up other relevant documents you may have, such as appraisals or even school reports. You should have a nice chunk of evidence from a wide variety of sources. Now it's time to examine it. Allow a few hours to review your notes and documents, preferably in one go. Note your answers to these questions; it will help you organise your insights.

1. What strikes you?

2. What surprises you?

3. What themes can you see that repeat from all the different sources?

4. What additional success stories have you been able to add?

5. What have you left behind – and are glad you have!?

6. What (and maybe whom) would you like to reconnect with?

7. What are you most proud of?

8. What has the process (not the content) of gathering the evidence taught you?

9. What, if anything, seems to be missing or absent from this valuable information?

10. How are you feeling?

And here's a question to ponder: if you met this person you're now reading about (you!), what would you think? Make a note of your insights, aha moments and reflections.

Summary: where are you now?

1. Doing a personal inventory, or stock-take, of your achievements, skills and strengths is a really worthwhile investment of your time.

2. There are heaps of different assessments you can try to identify your skills and strengths. It's worth finding out which tools your employer favours and having a go at them if you can.

3. Just because we find something easy to do doesn't mean that everyone else does. That which comes easily to us is often a strength.

4. Asking family and friends for their input is a great place to start. You'll be building your bravery muscles just asking, and getting accustomed to hearing people talk to you about you.

5. All this self-assessment, digging up the past, and talking to people about yourself can be emotional. Notice the feelings that you experience, which themselves are priceless feedback.

Now you're in a strong position to start looking at the future.

Resources

Skills and capability tests

http://www.bbc.co.uk/skillswise offers numeracy and literacy tests.

www.mensa.org.uk 'The high IQ Society', so you can probably guess the kind of test on offer (for a small fee).

https://nationalcareersservice.direct.gov.uk This is a great site for people of all ages and academic levels. To access the skills assessments, select the Career Tools tab then choose Skills Health Check Tools and select tests appropriate for your education level (it goes up to PhD, so there are some pretty stiff tests). There's a range of tools, including working with numbers, solving abstract problems and working with written information. Free access and downloadable reports.

http://www.shldirect.com/en is global talent assessment company CEB-SHL's test preparation site, offering free and paid-for practice tests.

Psychometric tools

www.bps.org.uk Home of the British Psychological Society. Head for the 'Psychology and the public' tab and then 'Information for the public' which includes resources such as 'What's in a psychometric test?' The excellent research digest blog is accessible to all.

http://www.psychometricinstitute.co.uk Has free practice psychometric assessments and aptitude tests.

It also sells online courses offering more in-depth practice and help for those about to take assessments.

http://www.teamtechnology.co.uk/ offers a free 'Mental Muscle Diagram Indicator™', based on Myers Briggs theory (behind the Myers Briggs Type Indicator® or MBTI). Detailed reports based on your MMDI are available for a small fee.

Strengths assessments

http://www.authentichappiness.sas.upenn.edu/questionnaires.aspx This is the University of Pennsylvania's Positive Psychology Center site, which offers heaps of free questionnaires. Registration required. I recommend the VIA Signature Strengths questionnaire.

http://www.cappeu.com/Realise2.aspx CAPP is the Centre for Applied Positive Psychology and Realise2 is their strengths assessment and development tool, used by major organisations. Individuals can complete their own Realise2 questionnaire online and get a report for a small fee. Check out the resources section of the website for free downloads and book sample chapters. I also recommend CAPP's books.

www.gallupstrengthscenter.com Here you can take the popular Clifton Strengthsfinder for a small fee.

CHAPTER 3

WHERE DO YOU WANT TO BE?

The previous two chapters may lead you directly to where you want to be. If so, great. Or you may be getting some ideas and clues. The three activities that follow will help you get clarity and set goals for the long and short term:

- Get clear on your values
- Look at the long, long term
- Set short-term goals

1. Get clear on your values

Before we get too carried away with where we want to get to, we need to install some essential sat-nav for the journey. Whether you're in your first or tenth year of work, you need integrity. We all have it, but some people seem to lose a little each step of the way as they progress in their careers, which is a real shame. To make sure you have integrity and hang onto it, identify what's important to you. Another way of putting this is being clear on your values. They span all areas of your life; it's not as though there's a work you and a weekend, off-duty you. You need to take your real self to work and to be confident about that you need to get clear on your values.

My advice is to simply dive into this next exercise with an open mind and an open heart. It can be done in half an hour, or you may want to take longer. As soon as you start analysing and thinking hard about it, you're at risk of putting down what you think might be 'the right answer', and if there is such a thing in this exercise, it's simply what's true for you. You're not being asked to write some cheesy corporate charter here. It's entirely up to you whether or not you share this with other people or keep it close to your chest. When you've done the exercise, I'll share with you the ways in which our values can be useful.

Your Values Statement

First, brainstorm all the answers that come into your head when you consider this question: what's really important to you? Start writing now!

Second, just in case you've missed something, or if you've got a little stuck, add words from the list below to your values.

Honesty   Integrity   Trust   Respect for the environment   Creativity   Love   Safety   Friendship   Freedom of expression   Passion   Adventure   Persistence   Love of nature   Curiosity   Family   Religion   Love of learning   Spirituality   Open-mindedness   Hard work   Innovation   Respect   New discoveries   Tradition   Helping others   Compassion   Achievement   Recognition   Fairness   Equality   Home   Peace & Quiet   Relaxation   Opportunity   Autonomy   Responsibility   Diversity   Originality   Energy   Commitment   Stability   Goal-focused   Companionship   Service to society

Now take a look at your values; the things that really matter to you. Identify your top three to five. You may find that tough to do if they're all important to you. If so, write each one on a card or Post-It and try ranking them, moving them around, deciding if this one is more important to you than another. Craft simple sentences that say what your top three to five values are and why they matter to you. Here's a structure to follow to help get you started.

I believe that [value goes here] is important because
. . . .

You've got your values – now what?

What's the point in getting clear on your values? I think it's important because many of us can fall into a trap of sleep-walking through our lives without being fully aware of our values, and it's only when they get violated in some way that we become aware of them. That might show up as getting overly upset by another person's behaviour towards us, or as something we feel strongly about and decide to take a stand on, and it can show up as guilt which can corrode our well-being because we're doing something that isn't true to our values.

Take a look back at your values right now, and think about times in your life when your values have taken a knock in some way, whether it was something you did that was out of line with them, or something that someone else did, or simply something that happened. How did that affect you? How did you feel at the time? What did you do/not do as a result? How do you feel about the situation now?

Getting clear on your values will act as your personal sat-nav for all kinds of things you do and say every day. When we behave in a way that's aligned to what we believe is important, we're being true to who we are.

Behaving in ways that align with your values will ensure you don't fall into any traps for the unwary. Those 'tough' people we don't admire so much may have fallen into traps, but it won't happen to you if you keep your values in plain sight. The good people we do admire, on the other hand, can probably rattle off a list of values and things that are deeply important to them, and I'll bet they sound good to you.

So now you're clear on your values, here's a challenge: thinking of your top three to five values, cast your mind back to yesterday and ask yourself how you walked your talk and did something that embodies those values during the day.

Here are five ways to keep your values in plain sight:

1. Make a note of your values on a postcard and keep it as a bookmark, or pin it up by your desk.

2. Create a visual of your values and take a photo of it on your smartphone.

3. Look up dictionary definitions of your values and bookmark them.

4. Search for inspirational quotes about your values and bookmark them.

5. Find music that relates to your values and create a playlist that you can listen to on your daily journey to work.

2. Look at the long, long term

Now you're ready to take a leap ahead in time. Imagine it's ten years from now, and you're at a celebration with colleagues past and present.

You decide the occasion: it may be to launch a start-up you're part of, celebrate your promotion, your book launch, screening a documentary about you, your retirement party, or something else work-related.

One of your colleagues – someone you like and respect – makes a speech. In this speech, they talk about the qualities they admire in you, your big achievements, how you have overcome setbacks, as well as some good times and funny stories.

For now, we're focusing on your career, hence the stipulation you choose a colleague to make the speech. By all means repeat this exercise on a more personal level, with a close friend, your partner or family member. Take care of yourself: this can be a very powerful and emotive exercise, so it is best to do it somewhere quiet and comfortable.

Now write that speech.

"Can I just ask...
...should I change career?"

These exercises encourage some soul searching, deep thinking and a more far-sighted look at our lives than many of us have done before. So it's not surprising that questions like this can come up. I usually recommend the questioner starts with the job they already have. Look at ways to bring your values to it, discuss how each week's tasks will move you closer to that long-term goal. For websites and books to help you, check out the resources.

3. From here to there – set short-term goals

Now you've got ideas about what you want to achieve over the next ten years. But how do you get from here to there? Quite simply, one step at a time. You need to set some milestones along the journey. If you've got your 'journey to here' handy, use this exercise to continue it, otherwise just create this visual and get going. Allow time to do this: it can take a two-hour coaching session to become completely clear on just one major goal.

On a piece of paper, make a long line from here to there – from now to 10 years hence.

Now	half-way	+10 years

At the + 10 years point (ideally you've stated the year), note a few words that sum up what you will feel, what's going on, what you will have achieved. Only a few words; just the most important ones from your speech exercise. Do the same thing for the Now point. Looking at both ends of your line, some thoughts will occur about what you want to be going on by the half-way point, or in 5 years from now; write those down too. Do the same thing for a point at roughly 7 years as well, and at 2 years, and then 1 year. Now really drill down and get specific about what will have changed at 6 months, 3 months and in the next 30 days. Aim for three to five specific things. A few clear goals are better than a long wish list.

Well done, you're well on your way to having a plan – yet there are some essential steps to help your dreams become reality, which means turning them into compelling goals. Unless you do that, they'll stay as dreams, or worse, become sticks to beat yourself up with. So now, write down your aims for the next 12 months

1.

2.

3.

4.

Now use the following five questions to check and, if necessary, amend your goals.

Is your goal stated positively? I see lots of goals written in negatives, such as "I won't smoke again". Look at that sentence and notice what the focus is: 'smoke again'. Or "I won't avoid presentations" – the focus is on what's to be avoided or got away from, and so there's not much idea about what to actually do. "I will seek out opportunities to do presentations" is the same underlying aim, but stated positively.

Is your goal true to your values? Identify which of your values from the earlier exercise align with achieving this goal. So "I'm gonna get promoted and I will do whatever it takes" might rub a few of them up the wrong way. Or not, depending on your values. Amend your goal if necessary so it's true to your values. When your goals and values align, the sat-nav will keep you going even when it gets tough.

What success measures does your goal have? Name it to get completely clear. So if you're doing more presentations, how many? To whom and when? Can you see yourself doing this? Where are you? If you can visualise yourself achieving this goal, you are much more likely to achieve it. Borrow from successful sportspeople and not only see yourself achieving it, but run a full glorious HD movie of you getting there, including the soundtrack of what you will hear and how you will feel.

What resources will help you get there? Resources can be strengths, skills and attributes you have, and you'll be able to identify these easily from your earlier inventory and information gathering. Resources can be time, the right kit and the right place. And of course resources can also be people, so you may have a mentor or workmate to help you rehearse those presentations.

What's the very next step? Time to step out – what is the very next action you will take towards getting this goal? Grammar clue: you need a verb here, to name the action. 'Presentation' is just too vague. "Draft a presentation to show my boss" is more like it, as is "get a date in the next 2 weeks to deliver a presentation". A useful tip is to plot out several next steps in sequence, for example "rehearse my presentation three times the day before", so that you have a daily plan of action to get you there. But the key thing is to identify that immediate next step, the one that gets you started.

You should find that your goals become more specific about what you'll do and how you'll do it. Do this for all the goals you want to achieve in the short to medium term. Yes, you will need to revisit them from time to time – I heartily recommend you do that regularly. Not only can urgent stuff hijack your time and distract you, your priorities may change. But most of all, it's about staying on track.

Summary: where do you want to be?

1. Our values are vital sat-nav for how we live our lives.

2. The more we live in accordance with our values, the more meaningful and rewarding our lives will be.

3. Writing a letter to ourselves from our future can be a highly emotional exercise, yet it's also highly worthwhile.

4. Scaling up to the big picture future and then down to more manageable, immediate chunks of time is how we set the goals that will get us taking that all-important first step.

5. Our goals and ambitions can shift over time and with changes in our circumstances. So it's a good idea to revisit these exercises from time to time.

Well done for getting to this point. You now have a great inventory of how you got to here, where you are now and where you want to be. Now it's time to build the essential people skills that will help you be Zoomly at work and achieve your professional goals.

Resources

http://www.ethics.org/resource/definitions-values
Not-for-profit organisation that offers a long list of
values with definitions

http://www.missionstatements.com/ has lots of
examples, from organisational to personal, plus a tool
for you to create your own mission statement "in under
an hour"

If you want to take a closer look at your career path,
you may want to get hold of *Career Anchors* by Edgar
Schein. There's a self-assessment booklet and another
volume which deals with the results. I also recommend
How to get a job you'll love by John Lees.

PART II:
THE PEOPLE SKILLS YOU NEED TO SUCCEED

CHAPTER 4

COMMUNICATE FOR CLARITY

Because we can read and write, speak and hear, we often don't give how we communicate a second thought. "I got my job, didn't I?" Indeed, you must have been able to communicate verbally and in writing reasonably well to get where you have right now, but we can all be better – really. Now that we communicate constantly and in real time – with colleagues, clients, friends and family – we need to be more aware of how we do that. We need to pause for thought, dust off our defaults and install some new habits that will help us communicate with clarity. Clarity makes a positive impact, as opposed to communicating with vague and cloudy waffle, which makes for confusion. We'll focus on the main ways we communicate at work:

- Communicating in writing – a.k.a. emails and how to write them well.

- Communicating face to face – in meetings and everyday conversations.

- Communicating on the phone – including conference and video calls.

Communicate in writing – a.k.a. emails

I'm going to focus on emails because that's the default written medium for most of us at work. Yes, there are people arriving in the workplace now who've never sent one (they've only used their social media messages), but as all our client organisations use email, let's stick with that.

What do we use emails for?

That's worth thinking about. Sometimes they may not be the best medium for the message. It may be quicker, simpler and better build a relationship to pick up the phone or go and talk to someone face to face. So the next time you're about to fire off an email, stop and think if it's really the best medium for what you need.

Emails are great:

- When you need to get people up to speed before a meeting.
- To follow up after a meeting, conference call or 1:1 call.
- When you're dealing with people in different locations and time zones, who may have different first languages.
- To confirm a conversation between colleagues.
- When you need to get some information across to people in a way that they can read when it suits them and keep on record.

However, emails aren't so great:

- When you have to break bad news to someone. Better to do this face to face or over the phone.

- When it's screamingly urgent. Face to face is best, otherwise a phone call or an online chat.

- For saying sorry. Again this is best done face to face, or on the phone. A card might also be appropriate.

- For negotiating. The tone can rapidly deteriorate and get quite nasty.

- For managing performance issues. Great care is needed here, so better to prepare for a face-to-face conversation and then email afterwards. If in doubt, get advice.

Write emails back to front

Or upside-down. What I mean here is start where you need to end up. A meeting's going to happen tomorrow so people need to 'read this before you come to the 1030 Tuesday session on X'. A conference call is booked so people need to 'clarify who's saying what on our conference call'. A meeting has just happened and people need to know 'actions following our meeting and who's doing what when'. This may seem completely common-sense to you, yet it's not what most of us tend to do. Most of us write the other way round, because that's how we've been taught and educated.

You're not at uni now, so no bonus points for writing using a structure that goes something like this: hypothesis, thesis, antithesis, synthesis, conclusion and recommendations (still reading?). In other words, a carefully argued build-up to a brilliant point, with the big reveal at the end. That's great if you've got 10,000 words to submit to an academic who's paid to read it and needs to check you've done the background work, know your stuff, and can apply critical reasoning. But you're not at uni now. Writing at work is different:

- You and your reader(s) are being paid to do a job.

- Your reader has different priorities.

- Your reader has little time to read.

- You have little time to write.

- What you've written will hardly be read at all, most likely scanned through quickly and often not to the end.

Your reader needs you to get to the point – fast. Emails can be a real time-suck and productivity drain. We spend far too much time on them, often because so many are poorly written. And that's why you need to work back to front. So start with what's needed, and by when. Only when you've established that do you support your point with the 'why'. Use short sentences. Active verbs are good: produce, present, speak, talk, discuss, call, agree, make, build, examine, prioritise. We Brits tend to waffle and use adjectives to soften things up and gloss them over. No longer:

we're dealing with different media now, in a different environment. What's more, we're dealing with many colleagues for whom English is not their first language.

- Start with your main point and then explain and support it.

- Be clear on actions – what exactly is the action needed next, by whom and by when.

- Use people's names. If Dan has to do something, use Dan's name at the start of the sentence. No, you're not dictating, you're being clear.

- Be nice – say please and thank you.

- Use your formatting tools, especially bullets and numbered points (check that your numbered items reflect their ranking in terms of importance, not just the order in which they occurred to you).

- Use sub-heads for your skim-readers. Use bold type and underline to separate text.

- Keep the word count short, and your sentences short. It's OK for your email to look long, provided it's well laid-out, crystal clear and easy to read. Better this than a dense block of text. If you've got a hefty word count, put it in an attachment.

- Go easy on the emoticons and exclamation marks.

Exercise: deliver great email

Go into your email system and find a fairly long and detailed email you have written. Apply the above tips to it, starting with the subject line. Write it back to front (or upside down). Re-format it and edit.

Now read both from the perspective of the recipient(s) and notice how you respond differently to each one.

Communicate face to face

Meetings

Let's start with meetings, and let's be clear: they could easily take up a whole book. Meetings are up there with emails when it comes to hijacking huge chunks of our precious time. "I seem to spend my life in meetings" is a commonly heard complaint. Of course, meetings are important; they're how we discuss and agree the stuff that needs to get done. However, I think they're often poorly run and take longer than they should. You've heard the wisdom about adding up the hourly rate of everyone in the room and multiplying that by the number of hours the meeting took – and if you haven't, just try it at your next meeting. Meetings are another productivity – and therefore profit – drain, and for many of us a source of frustration. We're thinking about what else we could be doing, what's going to be waiting for us when we get back to our desk, and what we'll have for lunch. Eventually, we're thinking about anything but the meeting we're in.

We work with lots of organisations and see some interesting ways of doing meetings. One of our clients has a firm rule of no meeting taking more than 45 minutes. Another has a similar rule – but for them the time limit is shorter. It took me a little while to cotton on, but as people started to gather their things at the 25-minute point, one of them saw my expression and told me; "It's a rule here: all meetings must be wrapped up at 30 minutes." They're a very successful company, so there must be something in it. Another Zoomly client has an area with high tables at which there's no choice but to stand – which keeps meetings short and sweet.

This is going to sound very old school, but you need an agenda for all your meetings – otherwise, what are you all doing with your precious time? At the top of the agenda needs to be how long the meeting will take. The agenda should be based on clear objectives. Even informal meetings need a reason why they're happening. What needs to have happened by the end of the meeting? Don't be coy about this: if you need to get approval on a budget, say so, in writing, where everyone can see it.

Respect each other's time and allocate time to each point you need to cover.

Use flip boards or whiteboards to capture actions publicly. I see lots of these used for illustrating ideas, which is great. They should also be used to be explicit about what's happening next, who's doing it and by when – written large and where everyone can see it. You'd be amazed how many people leave meetings unclear about what was agreed and who's doing it. That's a senseless waste of time and talent. If you want to take a more active role in meetings, offer to write up the action points as they are discussed and agreed, then summarise them at the end. Grab a photo of them on your smartphone and send it to the participants afterwards with your key points in the email. Do this quickly and you'll make everyone's lives easier. Tardy meeting follow-up is another drag on people's productivity and morale, so get known for nailing this task fast.

What do you say in meetings?

When it comes to what you say and do in a meeting, similar principles apply: get to your point quickly, and then back it up. Don't waffle. Stay focused on your objectives.

One of the best things you can do in meetings is listen really intently and make detailed notes; these two seemingly obvious things will put you ahead of most other people in the room, who probably do neither of them especially well. Once you start doing that, questions will occur to you – ask them. If you have a question about what someone means, or what the implications of their suggestion are, chances are you're not alone. If you don't understand something, at least one other person in the room probably doesn't either. So when you speak up, ask a clear question to check you understand what's going on, such as:

"Please can I make sure I've understood this correctly for our meeting notes – you want to launch in seven markets?"

"Can I just check I've got this – do you mean bring the start date forward two or three months?"

"Of these five objectives, what would you say are the priorities?"

"Can I just ask...

...I've been told to speak up more in meetings, but I have no idea what to say! How can I do this without looking an idiot?"

I'm asked this question a lot. You're not alone: in the babble that is most organisational meetings, it can seem a wise move for the less experienced to keep your head down. Then someone tells you that it's time to speak up – but what to say in amongst all that waffle, posturing, gibberish and nonsense? You imagine the whole room falling silent as everyone turns to look at you, clearly thinking 'What on EARTH are they on about!?'

Asking questions can be a real 'get out of jail free card' here. Offer to take the meeting notes so you have an active role in the meeting; a reason to be there. That will give you the right to ask questions to check you've got something down correctly. You then have a choice: open or closed questions.

Closed questions are so called because the recipient can only answer 'yes' or 'no' – their options are closed down. Closed questions tend to be 'Is it a this or a that?' or 'Did you say this or that?' or 'Would you be happy if we got it to you by Wednesday instead?' – they're handy for checking you've understood correctly, and for summarising.

Open questions are more likely to 'open up' the recipient and get a fuller answer. For example:

'How will you measure success?'

'What will make the biggest difference?'

'How many markets are involved?'

'What are the risks of doing that?'

Start with a few open and closed questions and notice the responses you get. Listen carefully to other people's questions: some can make meetings go round in circles; others can move things along brilliantly.

Deal with interruptions

Normal conversations often have what's called 'overlapping speech'; when one person talks at the same time as another, maybe echoing or agreeing with their point. Some people just can't help thinking aloud in response to another person as they speak. Overlapping which demonstrates active listening can encourage dialogue. Joining in when the speaker pauses at the end of a point is normal. Cutting across someone mid-sentence and breaking the flow of discussion is a different matter. Interrupters don't usually mean to be rude but the speaker may infer they are. Don't let that person be you; wait for your turn, raising a hand if necessary.

What if you're the one being interrupted? First of all, the statistics show you're far more likely to be a woman. This is well documented, and has been pointed out by high-profile women such as Sheryl Sandberg (can you imagine interrupting Facebook's CEO? Me neither). Watch your body language – no huffing, puffing, slamming your pen down or eye-rolling – stay focused on your interrupter whilst maintaining friendly eye contact and don't look down. Say "May I finish?" with a smile and then do so graciously. Do this every time someone interrupts you, which if you're a woman will be a lot. You'll be doing everyone a huge favour by raising awareness of this behaviour.

Chairing meetings

If you've ever been in a really well-run meeting, you will know that chairing meetings is an art – and it's one that's valued. Once you get used to speaking up in meetings, listening well and taking notes, asking relevant questions and taking a more active role, consider stepping up. You don't have to be the most senior person in the room to chair the meeting; you do have to be integral to the project under discussion and able to marshal the resources in the room. When you're making headway and contributing to meetings, ask your manager if you can start chairing some.

Everyday conversations

Mostly, unless someone pounces on you for your detailed point of view on your area of expertise, it's good to keep what you say short and sweet. Listen to people who've been trained to face the media and you'll notice they tend to use shorter sentences and end on a powerful take-away point. If footballers can master this art, so can you. Ditch the waffle, but not the niceties. Remember to say please and thank you. Show sincere consideration for another's point of view. And smile.

Communicate on the phone

That object on your desk with the curly wire joining a box to a receiver is increasingly relegated to third place behind the deluge of emails and the swamp of meetings. Which is a pity, as it can be an amazing tool. Pick up the phone and talk to someone and you can:

- Save time by avoiding endless email ping-pong.

- Avoid misunderstandings.

- Nip problems in the bud.

- Calm things down.
- Get an answer to your question, fast.
- Build better business relationships.

A phone call can be far better than an email when it comes to saying sorry, if you can't be there in person.

If you're making the call, prepare for it: have an objective or end point in mind. Make notes or a mind map of what you want to cover and the questions you will ask to get the answers you need. Anticipate the questions you'll be asked or the objections you could meet, and come up with ways to handle them.

You do answer your phone, don't you? I know a Managing Director who ran a short, frustrated tutorial for six employees whose 'You've got voice-mail' lights were left flashing for days on end.

If you're receiving the call, make notes of the key points. Take a breath before leaping in with your response or point of view, making sure you hear the speaker's point clearly. If you don't know the answer to something, say so, and say when you'll get back to the person. End the call well, with a summing-up of what's been agreed and who's doing what by when. Follow up on all calls requiring action with a quick email if other people need to know what's going on.

Conference and video calls

You're probably familiar with the squawk box in the middle of the table. Web-enabled meeting tools such as WebEx have improved the experience for most of us, but I suspect are under-used. The dynamics are very different when we can see each other on the call. Two things I've found with these calls are that a) they tend to be more abrupt than face-to-face conversation (which might be a good thing, or not), and b) a lot can go unsaid.

To help web-enabled meetings be more harmonious and productive, it helps to have a clearly identified chairperson for the call. This person is probably the most senior member of the team initiating the call, and they need to lead the discussion vigorously and rigorously.

Establish some basic etiquette:

- Have a list of all attendees' names and ensure that all parties know who is on the call. If you're using a web-based system, it can do this for you, but it's worth checking if people are sharing a terminal.

- If your system allows you to record the call and circulate it afterwards, make sure everyone knows it will be recorded.

- Establish how much time you have and restate the objective for the call.

- Clarify ground rules, such as when Q&A will

happen, requesting all contributors to be clear and concise, with no interruptions.

- Use people's names to identify whose contribution you want, or who needs to take the next step.

- If someone gets interrupted, make sure you go back to them by name to check their point has been made and heard (and by doing so, the interrupter will hopefully get the point, without you having to say a word to them).

- Allow time for brief questions, even if this means a pregnant pause at the end of each agenda point.

- Summarise frequently throughout as well as at the end.

Yes, this sounds beyond basic. But no, it doesn't often happen.

Spare a thought, write a card

Don't underestimate the power of sending a card. When everyone's overwhelmed, communicating in monosyllables and emoticons, barking orders and back-biting, the quality of our interactions can de-humanise rapidly. Send someone a card to congratulate them, say thank you, say you're sorry, good luck or happy birthday. Or just send something with a handwritten note saying 'I saw this and thought of you', which is the point after all.

Summary – communicate for clarity

1. Use email well and wisely. Clear subject lines grab the reader's attention and make it clear why they should read on. Assume your readers will skim so make it easy for them to get the key points.

2. Get known for great meetings. Have an agenda, identify objectives and allocate time.

3. Taking the notes and asking questions to check you've got the key points right are great ways to get more involved in meetings.

4. Pick up the phone. It can save a ton of time and is a richer medium than email, with less room for misunderstandings.

5. Remember common courtesies: say please and thank you. Smile more and frown less.

Resources

www.moo.com/postcards create your own postcards

Check out Sheryl Sandberg's book *Lean in: Women, Work and the Will to Lead* to find her thoughts on interruptions. There's also a video interview with Ms Sandberg on www.hbr.com

If you want to learn from respected writers, *The Economist Style Guide* is a good investment.

Nervous about your grammar? *Eats, Shoots and Leaves* by Lynne Truss will prove invaluable.

CHAPTER 5

FOCUS ON THE RIGHT THINGS

We'll look at some really practical tools and tips in this chapter to help you make the best use of your time, including:

- Where does your time go? Take the Three Day Challenge.

- Decide what you will stop doing – and create your 'NOT to do' list.

- If you don't do it... who should?

- What to focus on – criteria analysis.

- Plan your time and tasks using Three Kinds of Time.

But first of all, let's look at why you should pay attention to this.

Tom Peters famously said that "management is doing things right. Leadership is doing the right thing." Now that you're moving onwards and upwards in your career, you need to do different things. If you've been, or are about to be, promoted, you will need to do different things now... or else! I've observed many a promoted person move up to their new role and take all the tasks from their old job with them, as though the job they now have is their old one and new one combined. This is not the way to be Zoomly at work. It inevitably leads to overwhelm, as the stress of trying to do everything takes its toll. Stress isn't an illness: it's a state. But if it isn't dealt with, illness can result, so beware. When we're tired, stressed and feeling overwhelmed, we don't give of our best; not a good career move.

Let's not beat ourselves up too much, though. Instead, let's take a moment for some self-congratulation: time for your 'Ta Dah!' list. A 'Ta Dah!' list is all the things you have accomplished recently, every single thing, big or small, that you have got done. Start with yesterday and list all your completed tasks, then keep going, back over the day before yesterday, the day before that, and so on, listing all your accomplishments until you have filled a sheet of paper. Now take a look. Yes, you DO get a lot done, don't you? Well done!

It's a truth not universally understood, but sometimes we are the hardest person we have to manage. Read the last part of that sentence again if you're not sure, because what comes next may surprise you. What you need to do now in your daily work may be very different to what you actually are doing, and what you believe you're good at. Take a long hard look at where your time goes, by taking The Three Day Challenge.

The Three Day Challenge

Step 1. Start!

Starting today, and for three days, keep a record of exactly where your time goes. You can log it on a spreadsheet, download a template, or use an app. Or you can just scribble on some paper.

Each hour, note down what you've been doing. If you've been on a 30-minute call that needed an email follow-up which took 10 minutes, then note that. If you've been stuck on a train on your way to a meeting for 2 hours, note that. If you've been at a networking event for 4 hours, log it on your timesheet. Oh yes you can; it's only for three days.

After you've logged three consecutive days' worth of activity, you can move on to Step 2.

Step 2. Analyse

Where does your time actually go? Are you spending hours on social media? Are you playing fruitless email ping-pong? Are you having productive meetings? Are you doing things that belong in your old job? How much time are you spending on work that fits your new (or next) job description?

Go through your time log with a highlighter and mark the work (or, the non-work, that you've been doing whilst at work) that has taken the biggest chunk of your time. Add it all up: how many hours?

Now identify the 2nd and 3rd biggest chunks of time. For

most of us, the top three items provide insights aplenty, but you may want to go further and identify your top five, in which case go ahead.

Now you really can answer the question: where does your time actually go?

1.

2.

3.

Step 3. Commit

From now on, what will your top three priorities be?

How will you ensure you deliver on your new (next) job requirements?

What will you devote the most time to?

Tip: discuss your answers with your line manager and check you're working to the right priorities. (More on how to do this later in chapter 9.)

Welcome to your job!

Decide what you will STOP doing

Check your time log from your Three Day Challenge one more time. There are bound to be things you've been devoting your very valuable time to that you need to stop doing. And if we were sat together, having a conversation about this, now would be the time that you'd say to me something like: "I'm too busy to delegate that", or some such objection, for which read 'self-imposed obstacle' to your own progress. Let's deal with these self-imposed obstacles right now.

'I'm too busy to delegate.' Do you know what? Unless you DO delegate, too busy is what you will stay, as your peers and juniors get promoted around you. Unless you get over this obstacle you will remain stuck in your present job, or worse, derail in your next one. So see taking time to delegate as investing in both you and the person you will be delegating to – you both benefit and grow from the experience. Putting in the time now will free you up later, giving you time to devote to the tasks that really are what your new job requires. There's a lot more in the next chapter on how you actually do the delegating.

'I'm too busy to train them to do this.' See 'too busy to delegate' above. Do keep up! Seriously, your people need to know how to do stuff, and in time they will be training others. So who would you rather they learned this from? You, or another boss who is willing to help them develop?

'No-one else does it as well as me.' Brace yourself: this is the task that you must, must give up, or you'll end up doing it forever. You risk becoming far too emotionally attached to this part of your (old) job, which will make it hard for you to see someone else doing it, especially if they do it well – which, if you train them right, they will. So make delegating tasks that you are attached to – whether for what they do for you, or what you believe you do for them – the top priority.

'I'm not sure they're up to it.' Confession time: I once said this to my boss when he asked why I hadn't delegated something to a certain member of my team. What was I thinking? Maybe I was expecting some sympathy, or maybe a pithy phrase with which to admonish the under-performer. Instead, what I got was a very steely look and the words, "Well, she's your responsibility." Ouch. But oh so true. Welcome to your job moment. That person's (under) performance is your responsibility. If this excuse is one you're using right now, by all means make your boss aware that you have concerns about this person's performance, but in the very next breath offer your suggestions for helping them improve. It may be that they need training, by you or someone on the team, or by a subject matter expert. It may be that they need to practise and develop the necessary skills, with feedback and support from you on how they're doing. And if, when all of that has been done, the person still isn't performing, then that's a different kind of conversation. But only when you've done all you possibly can, with your own boss's blessing, to help this individual improve.

Create your NOT to do list

Creating a 'NOT to do' list is just as important as your 'to do' list. I'd go so far as to say, if you want to get promoted, it's even more important for the phase when you're transitioning into your new role. Get it written down, put it up where you can see it on a daily basis, add cartoons and quotes if it helps you, and make jokes about it if anyone asks. Just be sure to check in with it on a daily basis to make sure you're not doing things that belong in your old job – the stuff that your team are going to step up to doing in your place. By all means share your 'not to do' list with your team, and give them your blessing to call you out when they catch you drifting back into work on the list.

As I've been making the transition from one-woman band, Jill-of-all-trades to someone who owns a business, I've had to take my own advice on this point, and still do. Some of the items are to improve focus and productivity; others are tasks that team members do. To give you an idea, here's a 'not to do' list I found from a wee while back:

From today I will NOT:

Leave my email on all day.

Write and edit all our presentations.

Issue invoices.

Check my phone at random intervals for no particular reason.

Set up meetings via endless email ping-pong.

Work on five projects at the exact same time, all open on my computer.

Have a 'quick look' at the news, which turns into 20 minutes.

Log participant feedback into the master file.

Make my own travel arrangements.

Chase late payments.

(and more…)

So what's on your 'NOT not to do' list?

Running status meetings?

Writing meeting reports?

Being late?

Preparing presentations?

Gathering data and information?

Competitor info trawling and research?

Allowing meetings to overrun?

Sending meeting requests?

Chasing people in other departments?

Doing the billing?

If you don't do it... who should?

You may have been saying to yourself: "Yeah Dawn, dream on, as if there's anyone else I could get to do the billing (or some other such task)", or thinking, "All very well for you to say, but my team is already at full stretch", or some other such excuse. Let's stop and think here about who else could and should be doing this task. The options may be broader than you initially think. Let's start with the obvious one.

Your team. Let's consider your individual team members, and broaden that out to include those above you. What strengths are needed to do the job on your 'not to do' list? Who has those strengths, or if no one does, who has strengths that are aligned with the ones required? For example, attention to detail may align with data gathering and initial analysis, or clear spoken communication may align with writing up succinct meeting reports.

Who needs, or is actively seeking, a development challenge? There may be a task that's vital to the health of the team (and the business) that would really help this individual take a step up. If so, let them at it! OK, at first it may be a case of you sharing the job with them and taking time to help them get to a level of competence where they can take it over autonomously, but that's fine.

Who is showing potential? There may be relatively inexperienced people who are showing terrific capability to take on certain things, such as data analysis and insight, ahead of the received wisdom about when people start doing what. So long as you take responsibility for their output and give them the support they need, let them have a go.

Who needs to improve in a particular area? The task on your 'not to do' list may be something that one of your team desperately needs to improve on. So make it a project for them, being clear why this is something they need to work on, and how doing this task will help them beyond the task itself. We're going to get deeper into delegation in the next chapter.

By the way, your boss may figure in this thinking. They may have strengths or expertise that you don't in a particular area, and therefore may be a better person than you to teach one of your team members how to do something. And it may be that your boss would be grateful for some 'reverse mentoring' from that person in return. I'm told this is very much the case where social and web-enabled tools are concerned.

Other departments in your organisation. This is how most organisations get things done after all: work is farmed out, shared and delegated to those best placed to do it. This much we know, however, sometimes we can get stuck in tunnel vision, focused on 'what they do' rather than 'how they are able to do it'. So think beyond the task and see the skills set. That's how I was able to persuade the Finance Director to allow us to co-opt one of his team at our client's financial year end to help us reconcile the accounts for that year's projects (a job I was told we had stuffed up royally in previous years). Be prepared to barter and exchange skills sets here – which can only be good.

Outsource. This is more common than you might think. Remember the guy who outsourced his whole job to China? Many organisations now outsource routine tasks such as payroll management or benefits and rewards. In the creative and media sector it's standard practice to get in freelance expertise, such as graphic designers and copywriters or researchers, as and when projects call for it. But there's much more that we can outsource, and very cost-effectively. For example, there are people on the other side of the world who will happily make your presentation a thing of breathtaking infographic simplicity in a fraction of the time it would take you. I learned the basics of Google Apps for Business thanks to a UK-based Virtual Assistant and a guy in Mumbai. There are folks who would be thrilled to source the venue for your next client party, brilliant coders in Estonia, VAs in India, MBAs in the Philippines. People who will quickly, accurately and gratefully transcribe your focus group's ramblings. Or find your beloved the birthday present you have so far spent three evenings trawling the web searching for to no avail.

As with any outsourcing, you can't just call someone in and run up a bill with them on behalf of your employer; a clear and powerful business case needs to be made. So, if you have a major presentation coming up, you need top-notch infographics, your team can't do them as well (yet) and IT are overwhelmed, and you know this firm in Mumbai can do the job for under £150 and have examples to prove it, you should be able to at least get a fair hearing. Aspects such as confidentiality (via non-disclosure agreement or NDA) and payment terms will need to be covered. Consider time differences and communications too – a quick Skype video may reduce phone bills drastically. This kind of outsourcing can take some initial investment of your time, but it pays off in the long run. It's been my experience that the best place to start is not by browsing but by asking one's network for recommendations.

Get into the habit of outsourcing things in your personal life, too, whether that's getting someone else to do the laundry and ironing, book your holiday transfers, or do your annual tax return. Why, when you are perfectly able to do these things yourself? Three good reasons. 1. Because it frees up your valuable time. 2. Because it develops the habit of good delegation – you have more people to practise on! 3. Because it frees up your headspace to focus on what is really important to you and those who are important to you, at work and beyond. There's a whole chapter later in this book to help you get delegation right.

So... what WILL you focus on?

When you've identified what you're not going to do, you will have freed up space – in your head, as well as your calendar – to focus on the priorities in your role. Time to prepare for a conversation with your manager. Identify what you believe to be the priorities, and draft a list.

Try to rank the items in what you think is the priority order. It can be helpful to do a criteria analysis for this, where you list your goals down the left-hand side of a chart and add columns to the right, one for each criterion or reason why the goal is important. Then for each goal, work through the criteria, giving a mark out of five, where one is low and five is high, according to how well achieving this goal will meet the criterion.

Here's a brief example to give you an idea. Say someone has prioritised four goals and decided on the four criteria shown here. As they work across the criteria for each goal, allocating a mark out of five, it becomes apparent which of the goals can add the most value and therefore should take priority.

Goals			Criteria			
	Add value to client	Low or no cost – time & money	Boost expert status	Build revenue	Total	
Pitch and win additional research project	5	3	5	4	17	
Write posts for the company blog	2	3	5	1	11	
Run the weekly status meeting	4	3	3	3	13	
Update competitors' use of social media	5	3	5	3	16	

But what if the person really loves writing blog posts? Or if they're not comfortable around data and research? That's why criteria analyses are useful: they provide a reality check.

What if you have no idea what the criteria are? Stop and think; you've got heaps of clues, such as the company's goals and priorities. What your boss keeps emphasising is important. Maybe the goals in your last appraisal; they form the basis for a discussion so it's OK to note what you think are the important areas.

Then sit down with your manager and ensure you agree the goals and priorities. Get really specific about HOW the goals are to be achieved, what your role will be and how they will be involved, and how you will involve your team members.

Plan your time and tasks

It's been my observation that many of us are great at setting deadlines, and many of us are pretty good at hitting them – somehow. But often this can come at a cost: of our time, energy, stress levels and sometimes working relationships. I think this is because we're not great at recognising and working with three kinds of time: Deadline Time, Duration Time and Diary Time. When we get the hang of these three kinds of time, we're much more able to focus on the work that will really deliver results, and we're better placed to deal with the unexpected.

Deadline Time

Deadline Time is pretty straightforward: when is the delivery date for the work? It's better to have milestones along the way for stages of the project, so that we can chart progress, check things are on track, and take steps to correct if we're drifting. That way we minimise, or can even prevent, last-minute scrambling about to the finish.

Duration Time

So far, so good, but what about Duration Time? I think an understanding of this is crucial if we're to hit the deadline and deliver a high-quality job, and yet most of us seriously under-estimate how long things can take. We can under-estimate the time it takes for someone to get back to us, for a team member who's learning to do their bit of the task, for another department to schedule the job into their frantic workload – let alone how long it takes to get the job done right. If you're a bit of a perfectionist, that will add dramatically to Duration Time and may be something you will need to deal with. What's more, there are all the everyday time-sucking things that we let get in the way: hours of email, social media updates and mindless drifting around the web.

Work backwards. To get a grip on Duration Time, you need to think in terms of the hours, days, weeks and months it will take to achieve a goal. The secret is to break it down into specific and manageable chunks of actions, otherwise you won't have an achievable goal; you'll have a pipe-dream.

For example, let's say you have a goal to 'improve the presentation skills of two team members by their next annual appraisal' and the measure is that these people will then be able to create and deliver their own presentations. If those appraisals are happening in three months' time, work backwards, month by month, week by week, and identify the steps along the way. Let's say that training and coaching these individuals, showing them examples, helping them practise different aspects of their presentation skills, means you will need to devote an average of an hour per week to this cause.

Or maybe you have a goal to raise your profile as an expert, by writing twelve blog posts over the next year, and to do that, crystallising your thoughts on what's going on in your world each month, will require two hours per month. Or that to reach a goal of having fluent knowledge of your client's competitors within three months will require you to spend eight hours each month, or two to four hours each week doing web research and three or four field visits.

By now you may be thinking; "Whoa Dawn! When am I going to have the time?" Indeed, and you'd be quite right to wonder. First of all, remember that there's a whole heap of things you're not going to be doing any more – because they're not your job, they are the routine tasks, stretch challenges and expert areas where others can (or soon will) do them as well if not better than you. Secondly, there's the other aspect of time to consider: Diary Time. This one's a bit of a personal crusade of mine, so bear with me here. As I've said, I think we're pretty good at getting our heads around Deadline Time. In my view, most of us have been hopelessly underestimating Duration Time or how long it actually takes to get stuff done, partly because of what the psychologists call 'the curse of expertise' which is when we are so proficient at something we can do it quickly and tend to assume that everyone else can too.

Diary Time

With Diary Time, I've noticed we play a different kind of time trick on ourselves. I call it 'Parallel Universe Syndrome' and it works like this: say you are working diligently towards your deadline. OK, you may have underestimated how long it will take Jeremy or Julia to deliver their bit, so there will be some overruns creeping in, but for yourself, you're on course if you can put in some quality time today or tomorrow. The only thing is you've completely ignored the fact that at first light tomorrow you'll be on a train to another city to have a client meeting. The meeting is likely to include a lunch; after all it's not every day you meet up with this client face to face. Then there's the train journey back, when you and your colleagues will alternate between talking about the client, gossiping about colleagues and catching up with emails. Eight hours gone right there. OK, what about the day after tomorrow? Well there's a conference call, which will need a quick team catch-up before dialing in and a debrief afterwards, and a supplier presentation. Maybe an hour for the first and an hour and a half for the second. So over two days you're unlikely to get all the time you really need to hit the deadline – unless you work really late one evening. Sound familiar? It should do, most of us do this; it's as if our commitments to get things done exist in a parallel universe to the commitments in our calendar.

It's my little hunch that our inability to realise we're doing this to ourselves is a major cause of stress. Stir in three or four hours sucked up by dealing with email and you have a recipe for long hours, low energy and a constant nagging feeling that you're busy – but not really getting anywhere. The only way I have found to break out of this miserable cycle is to take control of your Diary Time.

Take control of your Diary Time

You've now broken your goals down into actionable chunks that have mini deadlines on them. You've got a more realistic picture of how long these chunks will take. So now what you're going to do is... drum roll... put them in your diary. Yes, you're actually going to create an entry in your calendar system that says, 'field visit for competitor research, 1 hour plus travel = 2 hours total'. You're going to put 'coaching Jeremy and Julia on their presentations, 1 hour' in your diary. You will take 60 seconds to enter the hour it will take you to write that blog post. It's all going to go in your diary: train journeys, post-call catch-ups, the lot.

There are several advantages to doing this, and a potential downside (which is solvable). The advantages include:

- You will be able to look at your month, week and day and see how you will be working towards the top priorities.

- If something is not high priority – or it wasn't when you last discussed goals and priorities with your boss – then you may decide it's not worth your time right now.

- You will eliminate the flurry of scraps of paper, Post It notes and random entries somewhere on your smartphone apps and have what you need to do all in one place.

- Your colleagues, your boss and anyone else who's interested will be able to see what you're doing. Which of course is focusing on priorities.

- You will be able to look back over time and see where your time actually went instead of wondering, dazed and confused, where on earth it's all gone.

- As you create your diary entries, you will notice that other people will need to be involved in some of these time commitments, and you'll be able to ping them an invite instead of playing interminable email ping-pong.

- Similarly, if colleagues need to get into your diary, they won't inadvertently hijack a whole chunk of time you were going to devote to your pet project by booking something in its place. They will have to ask you nicely if they can do this.

- When someone asks you to move a diary entry to allow for scheduling time where others' commitments need to be accommodated, you will then need to find a different time for your task instead of it falling off your to-do list for the week.

- When you really get the hang of this, you will even be able to have mornings, afternoons, or entire days when you focus on a particular area: a client, a market sector or key people in your team, for example. This greater focus will yield better results. Alannah Weston, the Creative Director of Selfridges, does this and she holds her job down with a four-day week.

If it's so great, what's the disadvantage? I think there is one, but getting a grip on our Diary Time will help us deal with it. There may still be too much to do, even when you've delegated work to team members, other departments, outsourced to experts, and even your boss. If that proves to be the case, you will be accumulating evidence as you faithfully put your time commitments in your diary. Evidence that may form the basis of discussion with your boss, or department head, or the Financial Director or other senior manager. Just wailing 'I don't have enough time!' frankly doesn't cut it. Showing them evidence will help, if nothing else, to get you a fair hearing and some recognition. It may help you get a chunk of someone's time on a regular basis or even another team member. And if you're really focusing on your priorities and not whatever takes your fancy as it drifts across your screen, you'll be getting results, which will also strengthen your position.

Plan it all in

When you've got your Diary Time in plain sight, you will not only be planning forward and focusing on delivery, you will also have vital information for the task that really will help to synthesise these three kinds of time: planning. This is essential if you're not to be at the whim of every email, phone call or person you encounter in your working day. Taking time to plan repays the investment many times over.

Try taking 10–15 minutes each day to plan your time against your goals. Some people like to do this at the beginning of each day, others like to plan the next day at the end of the present one. Once a week, take a little longer, so that you can plan the next five days. As things change and need juggling, your daily 10–15 minutes then becomes much more practical, rather than trying to cram in strategic thinking.

Take half a day once a month, or a three-hour chunk, to plan the coming month. Monthly planning helps us keep our long-term goals in clear view, and we can then follow up in our weekly plans to find that half-hour that will be necessary in the coming week. You get the idea; the longer the time period you're planning for, the longer you will need to allow to plan for it effectively. And yes, I think it's a great idea to take a few days each year to plan on an annual basis. Some people prefer to plan alone, some with a buddy. A mix of both works for me; taking time alone to draft the plans, then going over them with a buddy to check they're aligned with my goals and the timing is realistic, then keeping in touch to hold each other accountable.

Plan your time and you will, on a daily basis, be answering the question that bedevils too many of us: 'When am I going to do it?'

"Can I just ask...

...what if my boss frankly doesn't care about all the late nights I'm working?"

Sadly, your manager is not the only person doing this. You will need to employ a clear head and calm demeanour to explain that you <u>will</u> be able to do the job by *x* (your feasible deadline) but <u>won't</u> be able to do it by *y* (their unrealistic and possibly inconsiderate deadline). Unless, of course, they agree that this new task takes precedence over these other projects you're working on. Don't give them a long groaning list of what else you have on; instead, politely and clearly ask if what they're asking you to do now takes priority over A, B and C. Explain you really do want to help, which is why you need their help in identifying the priorities.

Review to learn

As part of your longer planning time, and on a shorter, more frequent basis, get into the habit of reviewing. This need not always be documented, nor take ages, but I think it's an often-overlooked (yet essential) step in planning. As the old saying goes, "lessons are repeated until they are learned", and that's certainly true in our working lives. It's also very frustrating for your manager, by the way, if you persist in doing something that doesn't quite work and don't learn the lessons from the experience. The same goes for learning from successes. This is where reviewing comes into the planning process, because lessons are learned that can then be applied, rather than floating out there in the ether. Whether it's a big deal post-pitch debrief, or a quick conversation after a meeting, or indeed your whole year, the questions we need to answer are pretty much the same:

What went well?

What didn't go so well?

What have I learned?

What will I do differently next time?

When will I do it?

As you make managing your Deadline Time, Duration Time, and Diary Time a habit that becomes second nature, taking a few minutes to answer these questions will really help you progress.

Summary: focus on the right things

1. Most of us have a nagging sense of under-accomplishment; of too much to do in too little time. We seldom stop to look at where our time actually goes, yet this is the vital first step to focusing on the right things.

2. Creating a 'NOT to do' list can be challenging, yet it pays back in many ways because it forces us to focus on doing that which delivers best results.

3. It's worth thinking laterally about who can help with tasks. Rather than thinking about roles, departments and functions, think about the skills necessary to do a task.

4. Integrating our three types of time – Deadline Time, Duration Time and Diary Time – is the key to focusing on important priorities and having the time to get stuff done.

5. Even a few minutes spent reviewing each day will pay big dividends.

Resources

http://evernote.com/ lots of people swear by this as the best way to stay on top of meetings and multiple projects across all their devices.

You can also enter 'Timesheet' into a search engine and download one that you like the look of.

CHAPTER 6

DELEGATE TO DEVELOP PEOPLE

Please read the chapter title again: Delegate to develop people. Confession time: once upon a long-ago time I used to think delegation was about dumping the stuff I didn't want to do any more on some poor unsuspecting person or people. No one had taught me how to delegate (nor had I asked; the thought simply didn't occur), and I had experienced some wildly different delegation from my own managers. It wasn't until I encountered an enlightened employer who put me on a management course, and a hard-nosed commercial environment (where time really was money), that the pieces began to fall into place. My wish for you, in that detour back to my c.v., is that you won't need to make too many of your own mistakes. You will simply get off to a flying start and zoom ahead. We'll cover:

- Why delegation is good... and not so good (and what to do about it)
- Elegant delegation – essential steps to take
- Being delegated TO

Delegation Is Good

Delegation is a good thing when done right. That's because:

1. It develops people who can then step up and take on a task, and in that way the whole team becomes more efficient and productive.

2. In the process of delegating to other people, you are developing too, which is also a good thing.

3. Each time you delegate you are getting better at it, and becoming more familiar with someone's strengths and weaknesses.

4. It shows you trust people to take something on and get it done.

5. Being entrusted with a task is very motivating for people, as they can see they're adding responsibility and making progress.

6. Being delegated to means that a job has more variety as new work is added.

7. It challenges people to take on something new that may stretch them out of their comfort zone.

8. Delegating some of your work may stretch you out of your comfort zone.

9. Each time you delegate something to someone, they are getting that extra bit of autonomy in their working lives. A perceived lack of autonomy is a stressor; greater autonomy

appeals to our inner drive to progress.

10. The right people are doing the right work, so resources, i.e. people, are being optimised. The job is being done by someone with the charge-out rate that matches the level of work required, so good delegation is good for business.

So far, so good. Yay, let's hear it for delegation! But, hark; I hear a nagging voice from you… 'but, but, but…'. There are all these reasons why you can't or won't delegate. So what's that about? Maybe it's about the potential downsides of delegation.

Delegation Is Not So Good

There are some valid reasons why delegation may not be quite so good. However I think the people who make sustainable progress in their careers generally find ways to deal with these. Here are some of the reasons I've heard from thousands of participants in our training courses over the years, about why delegation is not good, along with some thoughts to help you.

1. People sometimes screw up. Too true. And of course, you've never screwed up, have you? Think about it; even if you felt like the World's Biggest Failure at the time it happened, you emerged wiser from the experience. People do sometimes screw up, but if you delegate and manage them right you'll minimise both the chances of them doing so, and the damage that might get done.

2. People do things differently. Indeed, not everyone will relish doing that competitor review in quite the same way that you did. They might tackle the information gathering differently. They may have different ideas about how to display the data. They – whisper it – might even have ways of doing the task that are not only different to how you did it, but are better! I have had the privilege of experiencing this, and have learned to smile and count my blessings. So will you.

3. People may feel too challenged. Yes, they may see the job you're asking them to do as a stretch too far. This will involve some coaching and encouragement from you, reminding them of the progress they have made and are making. You will need to stand your ground if both you and they are going to get anywhere.

4. "I don't have time to delegate." Granted, the first time you delegate something to someone it's going to take up some time, both yours to explain it and help them along, and theirs to get the hang of it. But – and you know this deep down – over time, as that person gets going on the task, carries it out a second time, third time and so on, the time you have to put in will decrease, until doing that piece of work is their job, not yours.

5. "Won't I seem arrogant if I start delegating?" This is a worry I hear a lot from people

whose immediate teams are a very similar age and experience level to themselves. In more traditional, hierarchical organisations the thought that delegating is arrogant is far less likely to occur. So let's be clear: dumping something on someone from a great height, leaving them to figure it out whilst you catch up with your mates' social media updates is pretty arrogant. And yet, so is holding something back from them; are you so sure you're still the best person to do this? Delegating something to someone so that they develop and progress isn't arrogant; it's common sense.

6. "They're too busy." Everyone is busy these days, and if you're reading this in the UK, you are probably all too aware that we work the longest hours in Europe. So you're probably too busy, so is your boss, and maybe the person you're about to delegate to. However, if you're working longer hours than they are, something's wrong. Or if they're not being efficient and productive, so they're working longer but not necessarily harder or smarter, something's wrong there too. Be clear about how this task is appropriate for this person, how it fits into their role and the contribution required of them. They might need your guidance to get their priorities right, to decide how much time to dedicate to the task. But if it's their job, it's theirs to do, not yours.

When we deliver our training workshops and consider the obstacles we put in our own way around delegation, I see lots of 'aha' moments in the room. This really is Welcome to your job time. Now that you have new responsibilities for delivering a, b and c, someone else needs to step up and do d, e and f. See delegation not as dumping on someone, but as teaching, training, coaching, empowering, entrusting and ultimately developing people. And developing people is now a significant requirement of your role. The buck still stops with you, but you will be handing over responsibility to someone else to get the thing done.

"Can I just ask...

...what about delegating to someone you're friends with?'

This is a tough one. You don't want to seem to be bossing a mate. However if you treat your friend differently to other team members, resentment will soon follow. So have an honest conversation with them and make it clear you will find aspects of this conversation uncomfortable. At the same time explore why you must treat everyone fairly and not be soft on your friends.

Still not sure? Then I suggest you go back to Chapter 5, 'Focus on the right things' and the 'NOT to do' list exercise to help you get the bigger picture reasons why.

Elegant Delegation

In an ideal world, you would be able to match the right person to the right task. We're not in an ideal world though, so it's more often the reality that people do the best they can with the strengths they have. How much time should you put in on delegation? It depends on the complexity and importance of the task, and the experience and capability of the person, which means there are no hard and fast rules about how long it takes. However, there are some guiding prompts on what to cover.

First: prepare!

Before you have a conversation with the person you'll be delegating to, you need to prepare. Lack of preparation is a sure sign of bad delegation. No matter how many times you have delegated this task, or delegated to this person, you need to first get completely clear in your own mind about why and what you are delegating. You need to have prepared clear answers to these questions:

Why is the task needed?

What purpose does it serve, what is it for?

How does the output contribute to the overall objectives of the business?

How does the output contribute to the team's objectives?

What exactly is needed? What's the end product?

How will the resulting output be used?

How long should it take?

Who's an expert on this?

Who will help?

How will you coach and support the person you're delegating to?

When will you be available to do that?

You will need to gather examples and specimens. So let's say, if you're delegating a competitive review to someone for the first time, you'd gather examples of recent reviews, possibly from your team and others. Examples are the simplest way to show someone the standard that's required. They may have their own suggestions and better ideas, which is fine – so long as they achieve the standard required. Examples are miles more valuable to the person doing the task than a long lecture from you on how you would go about it. Sure, you may need to outline the steps along the way, but when you do so with an example the person on the receiving end has so much more to go on. Examples help prevent the person carrying out the task coming back to you a few hours or days later with some really basic questions, because they didn't quite get it the first time round. So you've got the point: examples are good.

Briefing – not dumping

When you're briefing someone on a task for the first time they'll be carrying it out, you need to take a sequence of steps. First, it's vital to give the big picture; the way in which this task fits in the overall scheme of things. Why is it important? Many participants on our workshops start to blush when we consider this point as it's so often neglected, or worse, the reason given is the most demotivating thing a person can hear: "It's a shit job but someone's got to do it. I had to and now so will you." Stop and think about being on the receiving end of that one; indeed you may have been. How motivating is that? How fired up are you about taking on this task? Saddled with a ton of student debt, having slogged through your exams and fought through the assessments and interviews to get the job, how worthwhile does all that seem now you're told "It's a shit job but someone's got to do it"? OK, there are some jobs that are, shall we say, routine, even boring, but that doesn't mean they're total rubbish. Entering data onto an order system may not feel like the world's most rewarding task at the time, but if you know that getting it done right and on time helps the company's cash flow position, then it starts to seem a whole lot more worthwhile. Giving the big picture up front is noticeably absent when a task gets dumped on someone, which isn't what you'll be doing. What you'll be doing is briefing them, which is a class apart, and a crucial element of that is giving the big picture; the overview.

Crystal clear standards and deadlines

Ensure you're completely clear about the standard required and by when, with reasons why. If you've got your examples together, they will be really useful here. You may need to outline the stages along the way to the final deadline, to give the person an idea of what's required of them, and who else needs to be involved along the way. Does someone need to sign off on this? Do you or your boss need to see the output before it goes anywhere?

Get them involved

Good delegation is characterised by dialogue, not monologue. You may have been on the receiving end of the latter, stunned into a mute state of non-comprehension but not sure where or when to get a word in edgeways. And then you probably went off wondering what on earth you were supposed to do, had a go, got nowhere and gave up. If so, you weren't the first and you won't be the last. But please don't let that become your default delegation style. If you're briefing as opposed to dumping a task on someone, getting them involved at this stage makes a huge difference. Briefing is a conversation, so to get one going you need to ask questions and let the person speak up. Here are some starters.

'What do you think?'

'How will you approach this?'

'What suggestions do you have?'

Consider how often you will need to communicate and keep each other updated on progress. Do you want to be copied in on every email? Do you want a daily update?

Sometimes the person may be so completely new to the task they really aren't sure of their answers to some of these questions. You will need to be quite a bit more directive with a first-timer than with someone doing a task for the second, third or fourth time. Even so, ask questions to check they understand. Which means that 'Do you understand?' probably isn't going to get you a truthful answer. It's a closed question, meaning the recipient is closed down to a limited choice of answers: yes or no. And 'no' in answer to 'Do you understand?' is generally not considered a good career move. So aim for more open questions that usually begin with 'what', 'how', 'when' and so on, which will encourage the person to speak. 'What questions do you have?' will open up a whole load of areas needing clarification that 'Do you understand?' will not, saving you both time and stress over the long run.

When someone has completed the task a few times, this conversation will become more two-way and less directive, but it still needs to happen. Encourage the person to apply the lessons learned from the last time, for example:

'What worked well for you last time you did this?'

'What do you want to do differently this time?'

'How can we work more effectively together on this?'

Be prepared for them to ask for your help; they may need you to demonstrate using a system on your computer, or to show them how you enter data. Agree up front the kind of help you can give, for example; 'How can I support you?', and when you will be available to provide it.

Monitoring progress

As you will have agreed how and when you will both catch up on progress, you should be able to check that the task is on course. If things are drifting off course, ask them what actions they propose taking to get back on track. You're entitled to voice your concern, and they're entitled to tell you what's going on, for example:

'I'm concerned about the amount of work you still have to do on this. How will you tackle it?'

'When will you do it, between now and [the deadline]?'

What if they have heaps of work on and are really struggling? This is a common question that pops up on our workshops and it's true that people, less experienced people particularly, can seem to be struggling with their workload. Resist the temptation to take the job back from them. You'll be setting a dangerous precedent for both of you. The individual may get a short-term sense of relief, but may also feel somewhat humiliated. You, too, will end up struggling, because something on your not to do list is still part of your workload. This is why it's vital to catch up on progress and let them tell you – and show you – how they're getting on. By all means teach, coach and support them, yet be firm that this task is now their job, not yours. You're not their parent, you're their manager. Making sure the right person is doing the right work is your responsibility. Welcome to your job.

Review and feedback

When the job has been done, a conversation needs to happen where you both review how it went and give feedback. If you're lucky, you'll also get some feedback from the person you delegated to. This conversation may take a while if the task was complex, or be a matter of minutes if it was something basic. Long or short, this stage is essential to ensure that lessons are learned all round. The key points to cover are:

What went well?

What didn't go so well?

What has been learned by the person – and you – from the experience?

What will be done differently next time?

Being delegated TO

I'm guessing you have someone, or several people, at work who delegate to you. so it's worth thinking about how you can apply the principles of elegant and effective delegation to being on the receiving end.

Make sure you get the overall big picture view: where does this fit in?

What is the purpose of the task?

What is the final deadline, and what key stage dates and deadlines are there along the way?

What support will you need, and how will it be available?

What resources will you have access to?

What help will you be able to get, from whom?

What examples can you be given?

When and how will you get and give feedback?

A tale from a participant illustrates the importance of effective delegation – and of being delegated to. See if you can spot what was missing from her story.

The managing director of this small PR firm, on his way out of the office at the end of the day, asked our participant – we'll call her Stella – to prepare 'some information' about a prospective new client that he would be meeting the next day. Keen to get involved in something new, and keen to do some work directly for the MD, Stella beamed as she said "Yes, sure. I'll have it ready for you first thing tomorrow morning."

Off went the MD, and Stella wrapped up the task she'd been doing and started trawling the web for more information. The more she trawled, the more she found, including some juicy articles about the company's performance. Stella then headed down to the basement where tons of company information and research reports were stored. She rummaged around for about half an hour, digging out some publications, then went back up to her desk

Stella thought the thing her MD would most likely need for his meeting would be a presentation showing the annual report data, so she set about creating spreadsheets, inputting figures, creating charts and graphs, then embedded them in a presentation. She also included some of the headlines she'd found, some photos and other visuals. This presentation was turning into a thing of beauty, a masterpiece: both her MD and the prospective client would be really impressed.

When she looked at the clock, Stella was astonished to see that three hours had gone by. She emailed the presentation to her MD, shut down her computer and suddenly feeling very tired, headed for home.

The next morning Stella was on her way to work when she checked her phone to find a reply to her message from the MD. It said; "Thanks. Didn't need all this, just a topline on market size, their market share and key competitors would have been fine. Just need something to read on the train."

The MD had wasted a good deal of Stella's time, which could have been better spent working on a fee-paying client, preparing her own work for the next day, or simply going home to relax with her flatmates. Not only that, she was now feeling pretty demotivated about the effort she'd put in. Stella was also feeling cross with herself for not asking more questions of the MD, which she would have done had it been her immediate boss making such a vague request.

Exercise:
get set for effective delegation

Think of something on your not to do list that you need to delegate. Use your answers to the questions below to help you prepare and get your delegation right first time. You may need to do some digging to get all the answers, but aim to answer all the questions, even if it's with one word. For some questions you may need to have a conversation with the person you're delegating to. That's fine, note this and include it in your initial briefing.

1. Why is this task necessary?

2. How does it contribute to the team's objectives?

3. How does it contribute to the organisation's objectives?

4. What output is required?

5. What format(s) are needed?

6. What is the deadline?

7. What mini-deadlines or key stage milestones are there along the way?

8. How many different examples can you gather together? Which ones?

9. Who is the best person to do this?

10. Why them and not someone else?

11. What are their strengths and challenges?

12. How much experience do they have in their role?

13. How much experience do they have of this task?

14. Have they done it before or is this the first time?

15. If this is their first time doing this task, how long can you devote to briefing them fully?

16. If they've done the task before, how did it go?

17. How will doing this task help them develop?

18. What skills will they bring to this task?

19. What challenges might they face along the way?

20. How much work do they currently have on?

21. Who do you know who's really good at this?

22. What resources are available?

23. How do you want to be kept informed?

24. When and how will you review progress?

25. How will you know they've done a brilliant job?

Summary: delegate to develop people

1. Good delegation develops the person being delegated to because they learn new tasks and develop new skills. Good delegation also develops the delegator, who stretches their people management skills and frees up time to take on their own new tasks.

2. We can put an astonishing array of obstacles in our own way to stop us delegating. Failure to remove, get around or over these obstacles will trap us in the same role for months or even years.

3. Delegation initially requires a lot of preparation and time supporting, teaching and coaching a novice. That time investment gets repaid as your team gets the hang of tasks and you can steadily back off.

4. Aim for dialogue when delegating, to get the person thinking, questioning and engaged.

5. Effective delegation has a clear link to the bottom line: the right people, with the right hourly/daily charge-out rates, are doing the right work.

Resources

www.blogs.hbr.org heaps of posts and tips for delegation

http://www.businessballs.com/delegation.htm also has tips and techniques, often in the site author's forthright style

CHAPTER 7

TELL PEOPLE HOW THEY'RE DOING

When I say that "people need to know how they're doing" in one of our Zoomly training workshops, I sometimes see a few different expressions around the room. Some people are in the position themselves of needing to know how they're doing, so they totally get it. Others, sometimes more senior, can be a bit confused. Maybe the idea is less familiar to them because by now they're pretty confident about how they themselves are doing. Occasionally, someone has the need to point out; "Why do they need to know how they're doing? It's their *%$±+* job!" To which I reply; "Indeed it is, and they are paid to do it. And at the same time, 'how they're doing' is your responsibility." A welcome to your job moment usually follows. Telling people how they're doing helps them to be Zoomly at work too. Here's what we'll cover:

- The risks of doing nothing and why appraisals are not enough.

- Balancing praising and building – and how to praise people without being a total creep.

- Building people up with developmental feedback – 7 essential steps.

The risks of doing nothing

It's very risky to assume that people 'just know' how they're doing. Being told how they're doing, loud and clear, is a key motivator. When this is lacking, it shows up – in exit interviews. Time and again HR people tell me that one of the most common reasons for leaving given in exit interviews is 'no one told me how I was doing'. Not surprisingly, said HR people despair as talent drains away needlessly, leaving them with another recruitment brief, and the firm with a hefty finder's fee to pay. To say nothing of the productivity drop as the demotivated departer works out their notice, and their replacement takes a few months to get up to speed. Not telling people how they're doing doesn't just hurt the people; it hurts the business.

Also, it's amazing how often people have a totally inaccurate idea of how they're doing. Self-assessments of performance differ wildly. One of your team may be running some 'I'm doing just fine' inner dialogue, with their own inner cheerleader telling them they did a great job today, and should get a badge – just for turning up. Another member of your team may have a determined inner critic, heaping negativity on their own efforts. Two people in similar roles, performing equally well (or badly) may have totally different ideas of how they are doing.

We are all, to some degree, unaware of our behaviour. If we did every single thing we do each day totally consciously, we'd be hopelessly unproductive and very, very tired. We humans are brilliant at picking up a skill, practising and learning it, then filing said skill in the unconscious part of our brain.

You don't consciously think about how you walk, or power up your computer, or dance, or get your smartphone to do something; you do it automatically. It's only when something is new or a bit strange to us that we are highly conscious of how we're doing it. What this means is that we may become really good at something and have no idea how it happened – which can make it quite difficult to teach someone else, by the way. It also means that we may develop some bad habits when doing something and have no idea that we have, unless someone actually tells us.

Appraisals are fine – but not enough

"What about appraisals, don't they tell people how they're doing?" I hear you ask. Appraisals generally happen once a year, which isn't anything like often enough for people to know how they're doing. Also, when they're done right, appraisals should merely formalise and record the conversations that have been happening all year – with no nasty surprises. Both parties prepare for the conversation, gathering evidence of how they have done this or haven't achieved that, and drafting goals to move forward. When they're done right, appraisals are a positive experience, and far less of a time suck and drama than people perceive them to be – provided the appraisee has been effectively managed the rest of the year. Which is a major caveat, but I've seen this too often to believe otherwise.

Why don't we tell people how they're doing?

Here are some of the reasons people come up with on our training workshops:

'I'm too busy to have that conversation.'

'I don't want to upset them.'

'I'd be too embarrassed to tell them. Anyway, we're mates.'

'I don't know where to start.'

'I can't really explain what they're doing wrong.'

'I'd feel a total creep telling someone they've done a great job.'

'They're OK really.'

You may have said similar things to yourself, but now you know the fatal flaws in not telling people how they're doing, right? Just in case, let's sum it up:

Telling people how they're doing motivates them, keeps them on track, improves individual, team and organisational performance – and it's your job.

Still cringeing in the corner? OK, I have good news for you.

Seek a balance of praising and building

When you tell people how they're doing, you need to seek a balance between what I call praising and building. Each is a different kind of feedback. You're a clever person (you're reading this book!) so I reckon you can get what 'praising' is all about. 'Building' is the term I use when others might use 'constructive criticism' or 'developmental feedback'.

Personally I find 'constructive criticism' unhelpful as our focus tends to be on the criticism more than the constructive, human nature being what it is. The same focus may also apply to the giver of constructive criticism, which will mean the recipient gets an old-fashioned telling off. 'Developmental feedback' is OK, and a term much loved amongst HR and us training folk, but it's a bit like jargon for most professional people, and possibly too much of a mouthful to use in a conversation with one of your colleagues. 'Building' does what it says on the tin: it builds the recipient's awareness, skills and motivation, ultimately building their performance. Building also builds the trust and honesty between you both. When you build someone, you're building yourself as you do it.

When you get praising and building in balance, you will feel much better about having those sticky conversations when someone has screwed up. They will know where they stand with you and feel good about that, because you tell them when they're doing a great job, not just when they've messed something up. When you get praising and building in balance, you earn the right to have the conversation about sub-standard performance, and you will feel more comfortable doing so. So let's start with the good stuff: praising.

Ideal ratio of praising:building

In her book *Positivity*, Barbara Fredrickson found after extensive research that there really is an ideal ratio on this (find out more about *Positivity* in the resources). At work, the ideal ratio is at least three instances of praising to one of building. So for most of us, that means we need to be praising a LOT more than we have been. Many managers operate this ratio the other way round, and are shocked when we tell them the ideal to aim for. "What are we, some kind of cosy theme park or playground?" "Eeeuuuugh, that sounds really creepy!" It's OK. Praising doesn't have to be all sugar-coated nonsense. In fact, it's far better if it isn't.

How to praise people without being a total creep

High-fiving someone and shouting 'Well done!' is probably not what you have in mind for praising people. If so, good – it's not what I have in mind either. In fact, the overly loud, pat on the back 'good job!' kind of praising is only likely to get you a reputation as insincere at best. If you've ever been on the receiving end of that kind of praise, and I have, you'll recall how it felt at the time: slightly creepy. If you're British it would also have seemed rather all-American. Which is fine if you're a US citizen, but it just isn't how we do things in Europe. A major criticism I have of this kind of praising is that it's just not clear enough what the person has actually done that's good, and therein lies the key to getting praising right; it needs to be specific. Evidence is Good. Praising also needs to be genuine – you've got to mean it. The key to praising people so that you don't come over as a total creep is to tell the person exactly what it was they did that was good.

1. Get specific: what was good?

Think of one of your team or a colleague who recently did something that absolutely delighted you. Maybe they delivered their first presentation and it went well. Or perhaps they pulled a ton of data together in record time. This is important: what was it they actually did? Not what were they like, but what they did – behaviours. Grammatically, we're after verbs here, or doing words. Beware the trap of falling into adjectives, or descriptive words. If you find yourself thinking 'she was really proactive' or 'he was enthusiastic', you're not quite there yet. 'Proactive' and 'enthusiastic' are adjectives and they may well be accurate in terms of your impression of what the person did, but they don't actually spell out what they did that prompted you to form that impression.

Adjectives are unhelpful when it comes to telling people how they're doing for two reasons: first, the person is still no wiser about what they actually did to merit the praise, they just know they've made a favourable impression on you, so they are clueless as to how to repeatedly make that impression. Second, they're subjective; another observer of the same situation may form a different impression, and indeed the recipient of the praise may have an alternative view.

Verbs are the words that identify the actual behaviour that merited the praise. So your 'proactive' person may have 'taken initiative and looked the information up', 'conducted research', 'picked up the phone' or 'requested the meeting'. The 'enthusiastic' colleague might have 'kept smiling through a tough day', 'delivered their presentation well by using their voice and body language to convey their enthusiasm', or 'got on with their routine work and finished it ahead of time'. The idea here is to be crystal clear about what the person actually did, so that an impartial observer would be able to endorse what you're saying. This level of feedback is evidenced; it's not simply an opinion, and as such is much more powerful.

Think about it; if someone tells you you've been 'proactive', you might glow for a little while about the fact you've made a good impression, but it will soon wear off. You won't be at all clear about what it was you did that pleased them. Whereas if someone tells you 'you got the job done ahead of time', it not only says they've noticed and are pleased, but you know exactly what it was you did that caught their attention. The glow will last longer because you have firm evidence to back it up.

Praising specifically has another benefit: it can help both you and the recipient get a better understanding of their strengths. As you identify and praise the actual behaviour, you're making a mental note of something that person does well. Over time and with repetition you will become aware of them doing something consistently; that's probably a strength. If it seems to be something that comes easily to the individual, it's almost certainly a strength. And that's a really good reason to keep praising them whenever they do it, because it's all too easy for people to let their strengths go unnoticed and unrecognised, precisely because they are skills that require less effort.

2. Be positive: what impact did it have?

Someone doing something well may be unaware of the positive impact it can have, and as their manager you will need to spell it out for them. It's also good for you to do this, as it reminds you of the contribution this individual is making. So the 'enthusiastic' person who you will henceforth praise specifically because, say, they 'kept smiling through a tough day' will get to hear that 'it helped keep everyone's spirits up'. The 'proactive' team member who now gets your more specific praise that they 'picked up the phone' will see they 'calmed down a client who specialises in irate emails'.

Yes, describing the impact will need you to be sure of the facts – you can't just make this stuff up. But in the process of figuring out the impact you will be doing yourself and the person a big favour; linking their performance to the bigger picture. This is powerful reinforcement for you and for them.

3. Be sincere: what does it mean to you?

This may be as simple as saying 'I was really pleased that you...' or it may be a bigger deal, such as 'I was thrilled to see you deliver that presentation so clearly and confidently, because I get a buzz when people have a big breakthrough.' It doesn't have to be sugar-coated and schmaltzy. If the fact that someone got the job done ahead of time was simply a relief for you (as it's been a pain in the proverbial until now), then say so. In some way, on some level, you have a feeling about this person's performance in this particular instance. Our feelings are vital sat-nav for what's going on and when we express them in ways that are appropriate (as opposed to uncontrolled outbursts) at work, we're being sincere. If the most appropriate thing you have to say is 'thank you', that's just fine, so long as it's sincere and you're feeling grateful for that person's contribution.

Body language is worth a mention here: we humans can spot fake body language from a few miles off, so praise delivered with a wide-eyed fixed grin probably isn't going to be taken as sincere, and rightly so.

I think that praise is hugely powerful when spoken face to face; it's affirming for both parties and we can see how it's landing with the recipient. There are other ways to deliver praise, should you want to vary the medium or if the person is at another location. For example, you can send them an email or message; you could write a short note. The same principles of being specific, positive and sincere apply. However, I'd advise against going overboard with cards and flowers unless the person really has pulled out all the stops. It's not that I don't want you to show some love; my concern for you is more that you might be less frequent in your praise if it becomes a big deal. Little and often is far more effective and will help you achieve that 3:1 ratio far more easily.

The best way to overcome any residual fears you might have on this score about being a creep is simple: practice. The more you get into praising specifically, positively and sincerely, the more it will come to you naturally and simply be part of how you do what you do.

Sadly for many of us, our managers are unaware of the ideal praising:building ratio. You can simply decide it's not worth the risk to ask your boss for some specific praise for your work. They might take the request the wrong way, or you may be worried you'll open yourself up to ridicule – both of which are perfectly understandable. There are steps you can take to open up the lines of communication a bit more, and we'll be looking at those in Chapter 9.

For now, it's time for you to start noticing your ratio of praising to building. Yes, I know we haven't covered building yet. I'm asking you to stop at this point and consider your praising whilst it's uppermost in your mind. That way, you will start to raise your awareness of how often you're doing one part of the praising and building ratio. Trying to do both at once can seem too hard and you might put if off. Start now, doing this exercise before you go any further.

Exercise:
test your praising to building ratio

Thinking back over the past three days, make a note of when you praised someone. For each instance of praising, you need to note:

Person's name

How they earned the praise: what they did

How you praised them: what they said.

How many instances can you recall?

"Can I just ask...

...but what if I can't find anything at all to praise them about?"

This is probably because in some way, for some reason, you don't much like the person. They may be very different to you, have different attitudes, or ways of doing things. When that happens they unwittingly say and do all sorts of things that reinforce your unfavourable view of them. You have three options:

1. Look harder. There must be something they get right, otherwise how on earth did they get the job? This may require you to dig deep for examples, but please stick with it for both your sakes.

2. Isolate the behaviours that irritate you. You may be allowing those behaviours to infect your view of this person's entire performance, when there may be areas where they are meeting or exceeding what's expected of them.

3. If you still come up blank, very subtly and sparingly ask others. Tread carefully: you are not on a campaign here. So next time you're in conversation with a department head or client, at the very end just ask how they find working with this person. Their answers may reveal the good points you have been unable to see – until now – and you can start praising them. Or in the worst case, you may hear a poor review. Time to get some advice on managing this person's performance, so that you can agree what improvements need to be made, by when.

Build people up with developmental feedback

If you're working towards hitting the ideal praising to building ratio, you will have been praising quite a bit by now. Chances are, people will notice. In fact, you may find the whole praise thing such a shift it will take you a wee while to get here. That's OK. Or, it may be that you're finding the praise bit just too hard to get your head around and want to see what the building's all about. That's also OK, however you will find building far easier to do when you have mastered the key principles of praising. So if this is you, I suggest you take a look at this section then go back to praising and apply that first, then come back here.

Once you've mastered praise that is specific, positive and sincere, the potentially more tricky stuff about performance that needs to improve is much less... tricky. The same basic principles apply. People need to know how they're doing and that definitely includes things they're not doing right. Wouldn't you rather be told what you're doing wrong, so that you have a chance to do something about it? Or would you rather keep blundering on, causing damage as you go?

No sandwiches

Many times in our workshops when the topic of feedback comes up, someone says (loudly), "Well I've always been a great fan of the feedback (we'll use the polite term) sandwich. Y'know, a bit of good stuff, the thing they've stuffed up, and then some more good stuff to send them off on their way." An interesting debate then follows. Long ago and far away, I was taught to feed people sandwiches. Sometimes it worked and sometimes it didn't. Sometimes the recipient seemed confused; other times thrilled to be so highly praised.

Thankfully, someone put me right on the whole sandwich thing; stick to one point otherwise people won't know what you're on about. Human nature being what it is, when fed sandwiches some folks will only hear the bread bit; others will only hear the filling – and some will be just be plain confused. Over time, the praise gets devalued – 'wait for it, I know what's coming' – as people see through the whole sandwich thing. Little and often, with the balance in favour of praise, will help your people know how they're doing far more clearly than being fed sandwiches. Don't butter them up: give it to them straight.

So building, like praising, needs to be specific, and sincere. Unlike praising, where the positive impact might be described, the negative impact will need to be described if and when you need to help someone build their performance. Below are some other important points to watch out for when building.

What exactly needs to improve?

Be completely clear what this person is (or isn't) doing that is problematic, not up to scratch, and having an adverse impact on the team's performance. You may need to take care about this; if you're simply vaguely annoyed about someone's attitude, or fed up with the way they dress, stop and ask yourself exactly what adverse impact it is having. Is it damaging business relationships and if so, how? Is it causing problems for other team members and if so, what kind? Our own rights, wrongs and prejudices can surface when we sit as judge and jury on others, and there may be a very weak case in reality. If people are simply different to us, we can cut them no slack whatsoever even if they're doing a good enough job. We can also attribute errors to the person when other factors were at play. Yet when it comes to errors we make, all the other factors are magically crystal clear to us (it's called the fundamental attribution error, if you're interested). So as with praising, you need to identify in precise detail what the person is doing that needs to improve. We're back to verbs, not adjectives. So, 'You arrived late for the meeting' not 'You're sloppy'.

This means you will need to be prepared and sure of your facts. If the person's team-mates are complaining that they're not pulling their weight, you need to challenge the complainers for specific instances, when and what happened, and the impact it had. If a client moans that one of your team has a bad attitude, ask them to spell out exactly what behaviour led them to take that view, and when it happened.

When is the right time to talk about it?

Have a conversation about sub-standard performance as soon as you possibly can. Don't let the problem build up and grow. This will lead to resentment, not just from you, but from other team members, which can get really toxic. What's more, there's a risk you might suddenly blow your top when James is late for a client meeting for the tenth time. Not good. Nor is it good to wait until the person's appraisal, for a whole host of reasons, not least of which is the miserable waste of time and talent over all the time the individual has been screwing up before the appraisal discussion. Why wait? Also, it's bad practice (and bad manners) to spring nasty surprises on people in their appraisals. Appraisals should really formalise the conversations you have with people on a regular basis, and set goals for moving forward. The only notes of caution I would sound about having an improvement-focused conversation immediately are these: be calm, because if you're inflamed with rage by what you've just seen and heard it won't be good for either of you; and get somewhere you can't be overheard if you possibly can. Easier said than done in contemporary work environments, and we'll look at that some more next.

Where can you talk?

Loudly pointing out someone's shortcomings in the call centre layout beloved of so many offices clearly isn't going to be a pleasant experience for either of you, and I wouldn't recommend it. A little privacy really helps and shows respect. So what can you do? You can ask them to pull up a chair next to you and lower your voice somewhat. The racket is most workplaces should give you some cover. However, you might feel awkward and so might they. You can try to get a meeting room or quiet area and have a brief discussion there. 'But won't they think something's up?' Maybe, and so what if they do? You're not going to resort to violence: you're going to help them improve (which, remember, is your job). If you have a reputation as an ogre, people will rightly get a bit anxious if you ask them to step into a meeting room with you. But if you tell people how they're doing, both praising and building, and they know where they stand with you, they will be able to take it in their stride. Or you may decide it's best to leave the building. I'm convinced that chains of coffee shops have done very nicely, thank you, out of managers wanting somewhere neutral to have feedback conversations. If there's somewhere near you that works, use it.

How to start the conversation?

So how are you actually going to have this conversation? Here are the essential steps to take. I've given some examples, which I suggest you put into your own words as soon as you can.

1. Ask if it's OK to give some feedback at this time. Don't just spring the comments on your recipient. Even if delivered well, it's polite and much more positive to check they're able to have this conversation now.

It also signals what you're about to say and gives the person a chance to focus. You might say:

'There's something I noticed about how you spoke to the guy in finance. Can we talk about it now?'

'I'd like us to talk about your presentation. Is now a good time?'

'Can we have a chat about how you're getting on with Wendy (the client)? When would be a good time today?'

'I need to give you some feedback. Can we do this now? It won't take long.'

How you will ask if it's OK to give some feedback at this time.

_____

_____

Notice I haven't used the word 'building' as, whilst it works to explain the concept to people, it's unlikely to be the word you'd use in a normal conversation. But if it works for you, use 'building' by all means. Many people would use 'feedback', which is OK. 'Constructive criticism' in my opinion isn't OK; we just hear 'criticism'. Notice that these opening sentences are short and to the point: don't dress them up or beat about the bush.

2. State what you, or other people, have observed.
It's absolutely vital that you stick to the facts. This is why preparation is so important. You need to have prepared what you're going to say – the words – and how you're going to say it – the spoken words. The latter part is just as important so that you can be confident in what you're saying, rather than awkwardly blurting it out. You might say:

'I noticed you raised your voice at Kevin, and told him to 'Stop bugging me about the bloody timesheets'.

'Louise told me you were unable to answer some of the questions in that presentation.'

'Wendy has told me that you interrupted her several times in yesterday's meeting, in front of her team.'

'You've been late every morning this week.'

How you will state what you or other people have observed.

_____

_____

Notice that this hasn't been dressed up or sweetened, but is simply a statement of either observed behaviour or a relay of another's account of behaviour. Again, it's short and to the point, and uses language that is as neutral as is humanly possible.

3. Ask the recipient for their view. The idea here is that you check it's OK to say what you have observed, say it and then swiftly get the recipient involved in the conversation. This isn't a rant or monologue. The sooner the recipient is involved, the sooner you will both be able to resolve the situation. They need to be given fair hearing, so it's time to hand them the mic. You might say:

'So what's up with you and Kevin?'

'I've only got Louise's version so far, and I'd like to hear yours. What do you think happened?'

'So tell me what happened with you and Wendy.'

'So what's up?'

How you will ask the recipient for their view.

_____

_____

You will need to be patient here. Responses could range from an emotional outburst to sullen silence. Many of us, the first time we get any kind of feedback in the workplace, seem to revert to the first time we were told off by our parents or at school and behave with a matching level of (im)maturity. That's why you need to have these conversations frequently, so that they become a normal part of grown-up working life, aimed at building performance, not attacking the person. If they go quiet, don't feel you have to leap in and fill the silence with words – wait, calmly. If they get over-emotional, ask them to slow down and calm down. Let them tell you what's going on from their point of view and really, carefully, listen. Take notes if necessary – particularly if it's this person's account of something that happened when you weren't there.

4. Describe the impact, if necessary. I say 'if necessary' because it often isn't necessary to dig any further into the issue. People often know pretty quickly that what has been pointed out to them is a fair point, and if it's been done respectfully are more inclined to accept it. If there's no accusation, but a simple statement of fact, there's no wriggle room either. But sometimes you may need to help the person understand the bigger picture if they don't yet see it themselves, so you might say:

'How do you think Kevin felt?'

'What impact do you think it had on our recommendations?'

'How do you think Wendy felt?'

'How do you think your colleagues feel?'

How you will describe the impact.

_____

_____

Notice a lot of this is about how someone else (Kevin, Wendy, whoever) may have felt, which might be another country to your team member. But the idea is to encourage them to try to imagine it; to show a bit of empathy and think through the effect of their actions on others. Again you will need to give the recipient a fair hearing and listen carefully to their account of what's been going on. You may need to revisit the facts once you hear their side of the story.

5. Allow them to identify the steps to take. They are much more likely to take positive steps and do something to improve if they identify the actions themselves, rather than you telling them. To encourage this, you can try:

'What will you do about Kevin?'

'How can you follow up on this?'

'How can you resolve the situation with Wendy?'

'What will you do?'

How you will allow them to identify the steps to take.

_____

_____

6. End respectfully and succinctly. Resist the temptation to deliver your sermon here. You've both done brilliantly if you've made it to this point. So smile, say something like 'Sounds good to me' or 'Great, I'll leave you to it' – and get on with something else.

7. Look out for improvement and say when you've noticed. When the person has taken the steps they said they would, you will of course have a clear reason to praise them. So stay observant and as soon as you see the improved behaviour point it out, positively.

Please note: it's taken me a fair while to explain these steps, yet the words themselves are a matter of minutes. When prepared and delivered well, these conversations really don't need you to dive out to the coffee shop, book a meeting room or adjourn to the pub – unless you think the combination of the issue and the person merits it. These conversations simply become a normal part of how you do what you're already doing, which is managing people so they are great at their job.

When we've run our 'How to give effective feedback workshop', participants whose first language is not English seem to get on just fine with using verbs to pinpoint the behaviour they're discussing. The native English speakers can struggle a bit, but they get there in the end. Once the grammar lesson's over, everyone gets the hang of giving feedback in this way, and they're pleasantly surprised at how quick, simple and effective it can be. We always send a short email after the workshop to remind everyone of key learning points to apply, and after one of these sessions a reply came back immediately: "I've already done it, and it's worked!"

But what if...?

When we run workshops on managing performance and giving feedback, everyone is generally fine on the main points and key principles. Then, when we ask them to practise actually saying the words, we often notice the anxiety levels rise, and we're often met with a flurry of questions. You may have had these very questions pop into your head as you've been reading this section. Here are the ones we get most often.

'But what if they disagree?' If you have followed the steps outlined here, there won't be any wriggle room. You will be giving the recipient an example of the behaviour that has been observed, and a chance to give their own account of it. You may come across individuals who flatly deny the facts; if that's the case you will soon know who they are, just from your everyday dealings with them. If you need to do some building work with one such, two things may help you.

First, carefully check your facts, asking others if necessary for corroboration or challenge. Hopefully you won't need to use the views of others to back up your own, but if the recipient flatly denies that, for example, they yelled at Kevin from finance, then you will be able to say that not only you, but half a dozen other colleagues saw and heard him do just that. You might also have heard from Kevin, or his manager.

Second, have the conversation soon after the event, so that there is less opportunity for memories to get distorted – and keep on having it, every time there is a recurrence. Over time, the evidence will speak for itself and the recipient, who may have been genuinely unaware that they were doing something, runs out of wriggle room.

'But what if they get angry?' Our shouter might respond to observations about their behaviour by getting hot under the collar and shouting at you; what will you do then? First of all, keep breathing and stay calm yourself. Get suckered into a shouting match and you're both done for. Secondly, ask them to calm down and lower their voice, and do this in a tone that makes it clear you mean it: slowly and evenly, with eye contact. Then exploit their response by calmly pointing out that this is exactly the behaviour you, and all their colleagues, need them to work on. It isn't acceptable for people to be yelled at in this way at work. Losing one's cool in the heat of the moment can of course happen in a business where the staff are under a lot of pressure, yet we need to be mindful that others can be caught in the fallout. If the yelling persists at the time, ask the person to take a 10-minute time-out to calm themselves down, after which you will talk to them. If the yelling persists over time, or every time you have these conversations, it's probably part of a bigger issue and it may be necessary to consult your boss, department head, HR or a combination of the above to take disciplinary action.

'But what if they get upset?' At the other extreme, some souls may respond by getting upset, even reduced to tears. The best way to prevent this happening is to

get the ratio of praise to building right from the start, so that the person becomes accustomed to having conversations with you about their performance. If you know this individual is inclined to get upset, this is when you may need to find a quiet room, or go to that coffee bar (but please avoid the pub and alcohol!).

Some people really struggle with criticism, and if their response strikes you as emotionally out of proportion to the situation, you might be right. For some, feedback that points out an area where they're short of the standard cuts really deep, to a place way back in their past. You are not a counsellor or psychotherapist, so don't try to go digging into their personal history here. Keep the context of the behaviour in plain sight for both of you.

Point out that you're in the habit of discussing performance with all your team members and are always honest about what you see, because you want them to know how they're doing. That no one is singled out for special treatment either way. That by discussing performance, each person will know what they're doing well, and where – and how – they need to improve, so that they can progress. And that your team's progression and happiness at work are important to you.

If it helps, point out that it's only through others having these kinds of conversations with you that you have been able to progress in your own career. Don't let their upset state deter you from having the conversation. Allow longer if necessary, but ensure you get to the point where they have agreed the steps they will take to remedy the situation. And of course you will be watching for them to get it right, and praising them when they do.

'But what if they're my mate?' With the youthful employee profile at many of our client companies, this is something I hear a lot. With long hours and a sociable atmosphere, work colleagues can become part of our social lives very quickly. We develop a friendship, which in some cases can last long after working together. This can make life especially difficult for the newly-promoted manager.

Tough as this advice may sound, the best way to ensure you are still able to have conversations about performance is to lower the intensity of the friendship for a time. By all means have an honest conversation with the person and explain that you don't want to compromise your friendship, so for a while you will need to focus on the job and find your feet, which may mean you'll be seeing less of each other socially and may even mean having some awkward conversations. The friendship may not survive, in which case it was probably pretty fragile anyway.

I'm still good friends with someone who was my manager early on in my career and had to have several conversations to build my performance which were pretty tough at the time. But many years later we're still mates. If you're being paid to do a job that involves managing people and getting the best possible performance from them, there will be times when friendship needs to take a back seat. If you're now worried that you won't have a social life, then it's time to get in touch with other friends from beyond your current workplace and rekindle those friendships. Welcome to your job.

Summary: tell people how they're doing

1. 'No-one told me how I was doing' comes up in loads of exit interviews, and that's a real shame. Telling people how they're doing is motivating and helps them improve.

2. Most of us are pretty rubbish at giving positive feedback and could do with giving praise more often. Being really specific about the behaviour and the impact it had is the way to praise without looking a total creep. Be sincere.

3. Frequent praising is what earns us the right to deliver feedback that builds performance. Ideally we achieve a ratio of 3:1 in favour of praise.

4. We need to prepare for conversations that build performance so they go smoothly. It's best to be brief and stick to the facts. Ask a question or two to get the recipient involved and talking. Let them identify and commit to actions to take.

5. Make sure you end all these conversations respectfully. And when you spot improved performance, praise it.

Resources

http://www.positivityratio.com/ Dr. Barbara Fredrickson's site with more on the 'positivity ratio', an online test and of course the best-selling *Positivity* book.

There are some hilarious 'how not to' examples on YouTube.

CHAPTER 8

BRING OUT THE BEST IN YOUR TEAM

Your best team may be the one you already have. The perfect team doesn't just happen. People make it happen, and you're one of them. If you sit around waiting for the perfect team to land in your career path, you could be waiting a long, long time – which isn't being Zoomly at work. So here's what this chapter covers to help you pick up speed:

- How teams develop.

- Having a clear purpose, goals and roles.

- Establishing and maintaining team ground-rules.

- Working ON the team as well as IN the team – team tune-ups.

Think of great teams – obvious examples are high-achieving sports teams, but there are also work teams, such as start-ups – and what makes them great. There's usually a pattern.

They know why they're a team, and have a clear sense of purpose.

They know where they're going (even if they have no idea at first how they're going to get there – true of many bands for example).

They know what they need to do to succeed, and how they're going to do it.

There is some kind of code of conduct, norms about 'how we do things round here'.

They know who's doing what, who's good at what, and their shared purpose builds trust.

This doesn't happen overnight: it takes time, as teams have a development cycle, as do all life forms. When the pattern is incomplete or broken then so, sadly, is the team.

How teams develop

It is a mistake to assume that people 'just know' how to behave in a work team (or any other kind of team). There's tons of evidence in many workplaces that this just isn't so. From misunderstandings to major disagreements, teams can be a source of stress and upset at work. You may have been in one of these teams, and I'm willing to bet you have also been in a team that worked really effectively together, got through bad times together, kept each other motivated and succeeded together.

Why are some teams the successful kind, and others the ones that just never get there? The answer has to do with team development. A group of people thrown together and told to get on with it is not a team. The group has to develop into a team, and it may do so over a long and possibly painful amount of time, or quite rapidly.

First phase – Gathering

At first, the group assembles and it can be like the first day of school, with team members being brash and loud or shy and withdrawn. And just like early school days, unless there are rules, which are enforced with a dose of discipline, the group will stay child-like and chaotic. If you have ever experienced such a dysfunctional team (and I vividly remember one such on an unhappy new business pitch), you will know it's no fun. Clear goals, roles and ground rules are essential here (of which more very soon). Strong team leaders need to be directive at this stage, which for many new to the role goes against the grain. But try to be everyone's best friend at this early stage and you'll be done for. You aren't their parent, nor should you try to be, but you will need to take charge.

Second phase – Ganging-up

Once through the initial phase, what comes after childhood? I think you can remember. Enter that awkward teenager, who although they know the rules, seems to think their main purpose in life is to complain about them, ignore them and rebel against them. This stage is characterised by cliques forming, us versus them, in-fighting and boundary testing. So here again, as the team leader you will need to reinforce those boundaries, deal with conflict and call people to account. This stage is very high energy, but also takes its toll on all the team members. It's a case of reminding everyone of the goals, roles and ground rules, and why this group of people is a team. I've known teams stay stuck at this stage, still bickering amongst themselves as they arrive for a client meeting. And could the client tell? You bet – we humans have brilliant antennae for this stuff.

Third phase – Growing-up

If the team leader has been fulfilling their role, then the group has a strong chance of making it out of the teenage stage and reaching the next level of maturity. Think of it as moving into a first home, rather than an unloved shared student flat. So there's pride in being in this team – it is indeed now a team, much more than a group – and there's clarity about why this team exists. There's an acknowledgement of everyone's strengths, and how people bring these to their roles within the team. Instead of 'us versus them', it's 'us' and 'we'. Everyone is more focused on reaching the goals, and they observe the team's ground rules. At this stage in the team's development, the team leader can and should back off a bit, just as no new home-owner likes to be told what colour to paint their walls.

Fourth phase – Goal-getting

The high performance that teams are capable of is only fully achieved as the team reaches the next stage of development, when there is maturity and wisdom applied to reaching the goals. Debate is honest and open, no grudges swept under the carpet. Disagreements are aired and dealt with. The team leader's role becomes one of keeping the team in touch with the outside world, challenging them constructively, and making sure their great working relationships don't lead to complacency.

It's been my observation that really focused teams with a strong leader can get to this goal-getting high performance stage very quickly, and there are many others that never get there.

Goodbye

There's a further stage that can happen, which is when a team is disbanded, such as after a pitch. At this time, team members may get very emotional and experience a genuine sense of loss. If you've ever seen a bunch of returning holiday makers in a group hug by the luggage carousel, not wanting to go home just yet (ski holidays seem to produce this a lot), you'll know exactly what I mean. It's important to allow people to say their goodbyes, acknowledge each other's efforts, and keep in touch if they want to.

Back to the start

One final important point about stages in team development: whenever the composition of the team changes, it's back to the start. Yes, even if your team takes on an intern for three months, that's everyone back to the first day at school. A new team leader will have a greater impact on the team's progress through the phases than will a junior recruit, but it's important to acknowledge that this process will happen. How new joiners are inducted into teams is a very neglected area in my opinion. Lots of workplace strife could be eliminated if this were given some thought and effort.

Team tales

1. Think of a team you have been part of that was successful, and that you enjoyed being part of.

    - What was it like to be part of this team?

    - What did the team achieve?

    - How did the team succeed?

2. Now think of another team you have been part of that was very different to your first example. This team struggled and you didn't enjoy being part of it.

    - What was it like to be part of this team?

    - What did the team achieve?

    - How did the team succeed?

3. Finally, what phase of development was each team at? Next to each of your examples, write the phase that best fits: Gathering, Ganging-up, Growing-up, Goal-getting, or Goodbye.

So now you know that teams go through stages of development, how can you create your great team?

Have a clear team purpose

Why is this group of people a team? There has to be a reason or there really shouldn't be a team. This may take the form of a mission statement, or use business goals such as Key Performance Indicators (KPIs), Performance Objectives (POs), or even job descriptions. The team's purpose should be greater than the sum of the people in the team. Whatever the source, the team's purpose needs to be short and sweet, not a 10-page document, but something each team member can remember and say in a sentence or two.

Team members need to be fully behind the purpose of the team. Any dissent, or 'don't know why we're doing this' and you're all headed for trouble. For examples of mission statements, take a look at www.missionstatements.com. The success measures, or how everyone will know the team is succeeding in its mission, should be included. If these change on an annual, quarterly or weekly basis, then fine; separate them yet keep them in plain sight, displayed for all to see. Without a clear sense of purpose a team is doomed to be a random assembly of souls, even if the boss thinks there is some sort of reason why. As the saying goes, "if you don't know where you're going, any road will take you there". When you're clear on your team's purpose, you will then – ideally as a team – be able to answer the question, 'How will we know we are doing a great job?'

Have long-term and short-term goals

So you've got your team mission statement, a clear purpose. Great. Now the next step may at first sound like duplication but it's not. Mission statements are guiding lights, our 'why we're a team'. We need clear goals to aim for to achieve that mission, otherwise the language can get a bit woolly, tasks and roles are too loosely defined, and chaos ensues. This is about the 'what' and the 'when' of the team – what do we need to achieve, and by when?

Long-term goals may be five years, two years or more likely, one year. The timing may be a calendar year or a financial one, or a deadline for a particular industry date in the calendar, such as a major exhibition, trade fair or award entries. Goals need to articulate exactly what is expected and how everyone – not just in the team, but also in the wider organisation – will know it has been achieved. This means observable measures, metrics, numbers, percentage shifts.

Here are some examples:

- To win at least three extra projects from this client this year.

- To successfully launch four more products over the next two years, hitting distribution and sales targets.

- To increase profitability by 5% over the next three years.

Short-term goals are the steps along the way to reach the long-term ones. They help us stay focused on the bigger picture and chart progress. Without short-term goals it's too easy to put off the big push needed 'until after Easter', then 'until after the summer holidays', then until after... oops, missed the target. So this means drilling down into more detail what the steps are along the way, or dividing up the longer-term targets, so that twelve in one year becomes three per quarter, or one per month.

Here are some examples:

- To improve our first-time strike rate of ideas presented and bought by 50% within four months.

- To successfully launch product X by June, hitting distribution and sales targets.

- To reduce our re-work and overtime on this project.

Have clearly-defined roles

When the team's purpose and their long- and short-term success measures have been defined, the whole sometimes sticky business of who does what becomes much more straightforward. When you and your team clarify the actions that need to be taken to deliver the goals, you're well on the way.

A good way to approach this is to address the question; 'How will we know that the person responsible for

X is doing a great job?' Again, this will lead you to clarify the expectations; the results that need to be delivered. When you identify these factors as a team, it can be extremely powerful. If you can reach a point where each team member can say – out loud – 'I'm responsible for XYZ', you are getting closer to having that 'perfect team'. By the way, it can also be useful for team members to identify what they're NOT responsible for. I've noticed that there can be some raised eyebrows at this point, as in 'Really? Oh, I thought you were responsible for that!' So doing this can remove any lingering misconceptions and doubts, bring assumptions to the surface and lead to a more productive discussion about whether the task is that person's responsibility or someone else's.

> Two very different experiences of team pitches come to mind. The first was a bit of a nightmare: the night before the pitch, instead of rehearsing, there was a total panic as two members of the team (I was one) realised they'd thought the other one had briefed people to prepare visuals needed to dress the room. Verbal assault from the team leader ensued. There was very little rehearsal, somewhat less sleep and a disjointed team presentation. Needless to say we didn't win. The second pitch included regular team meet-ups that ended with everyone telling the pitch leader what they'd have done by the next meeting. We rehearsed well, performed well, and won.

Establish and maintain team ground rules

Experienced people can come badly unstuck when they switch roles or, worse, roles and employers, no matter how capable they were in their previous role. Sure, it may be down to lack of skill or knowledge, but just as often the person can be tripped up by not knowing 'how we do things round here'. Organisations have different cultures, and so do teams. A vital part of your team's culture is about the ground rules, which all too often go unspoken – until somebody violates one.

As part of the process of defining goals and roles, I think it's essential to also set the ground rules for the team. The team leader may do this, and say; 'This is how it's going to be', or the team as a whole may generate the rules they want everyone to abide by. The latter is more likely to get buy-in from everyone; however if people are just going through the motions and will then carry on in their own sweet way, disregarding the rules, then the former route may be necessary. The key to getting people to abide by team ground rules is to build into the initial process 'how we will hold ourselves and each other accountable', or 'what we do if someone breaks our rules'. And then do it. So if your team agrees and sets a ground rule for being in on time in the morning no matter what (because your client always is) and then someone is late, you will deal with it. Letting the transgressor get away with it, 'because I don't want to upset them' or for the sake of a quiet life, will pave the way for simmering resentment, and signal that breaking the rules is OK.

"Can I just ask...

...what if one of my team members isn't pulling their weight?'

This can be quite commonplace, and that's a pity, because tolerating slackers is corrosive for teams. Talking to other team members about it smacks of subterfuge and going straight to the boss seems like telling tales.

First of all, carefully observe other team members' responses to the 'slacker'. They may show some annoyance and frustration, or smile politely, or be friendly and happy. Do the same when the 'slacker' is in conversation with your boss. It may be that others feel the same way as you do. Or they may not perceive any problem; it may be that this person simply has a different way of working than you do, but they still deliver what's expected.

If your observation suggests the other team members share your views, tread carefully. Have just one very short conversation with a peer team member to clarify exactly what behaviour is problematic, the impact this is having and between you decide what, if anything, to do. Then have a brief, calm and clear conversation with the team leader (your boss) where you outline the problem and its impact and ask for their views on the best course of action.

Play to team members' strengths

This is a given in sports teams, but not as straightforward at work. However, if we are prepared to bring some maturity and flexibility to how the team functions, it is well worth doing. When people are making the most of their strengths they are more motivated – we all are – and when this is done within a team it can be exceptionally motivating as team members acknowledge and respect colleagues' contributions. Someone's shortcomings can be compensated for by another team member, who in turn complements someone else's skills.

I've mentioned strengths before, and it can be very useful to get everyone on a team to do an assessment of this. Alternatively, strengths can be discussed as a team, with individuals identifying what they believe to be their strengths and colleagues adding their views. It can be very powerful to combine assessments with team discussions of everyone's strengths, and how they bring them to team tasks.

Work ON the team as well as IN the team

Successful teams take time to explore how they are working as a team, as well as the day job of what they are working on. This can really pay dividends if done frequently, say briefly at a weekly meeting, or more in depth at a monthly one. Think of it as a regular tune-up to make sure the engine that is a work team is performing at its best. Here are some questions to get everyone contributing to what's going on for the team.

10 questions for team tune-ups

1. Why are we a team?

2. What are our goals and objectives?

3. What actions do we regularly take to achieve our goals?

4. What are our priorities?

5. What resources do we have?

6. What recent successes have we had?

7. What's working well?

8. What's not working so well?

9. What have we learned?

10. What needs to change?

End a team tune-up with each team member making a commitment to action that will improve the team's performance. Note the commitments on a flip chart. Start the next team tune-up with a review of the results those actions have achieved.

Summary: bring the best out in your team

1. Teams don't just happen: they develop. Some become successful faster than others. Other teams get stuck and underperform. A strong sense of purpose is vital.

2. Teams go through phases of development: Gathering, when the group of individuals assemble, is when they need clear goals, roles and ground-rules. Ganging-up is when the rules – and the team leader – are tested. Growing-up is when the team shows more maturity and takes responsibility to contribute to success. Goal-getting is when the team is really performing at its best. Goodbye is when the team is disbanded. Remember that whenever the team's make-up changes, it's back to the start.

3. Having crystal-clear goals, roles and ground-rules are the three essentials of getting from a group of people to a team. Goals are fairly straightforward; have long-term goals to aim for and short-term goals to maintain momentum. Crafting and clarifying roles can be more complex. And ground-rules can be uncomfortable things to create, but are absolutely vital.

4. Identifying and playing to individual team members' strengths is what the best teams quickly learn to do. This takes openness and flexibility.

5. It's important to work ON the team – exploring how well it's working, what can be better – as well as IN the team – getting stuff done.

Resources

http://www.missionstatements.com/team_mission_statements.html has lots of household-name examples of team mission statements for a range of work disciplines.

There are heaps of books out there on teams and how to get the best from them. My recommendation is *Effective Teamwork* by Professor Michael West because it's solidly evidenced and very practical. Professor West's work with teams in operating theatres has lowered patient mortality rates.

CHAPTER 9

MANAGE UPWARDS TO SURVIVE AND THRIVE

Think of all your relationships at work and then think of the ones that are really important to you. I hope your relationship with your boss is somewhere in there. Want to be Zoomly at work? This is the relationship that can have the greatest impact on your career, so here's what we'll cover:

- Identifying your 'who's who round here' and what makes them tick.

- Handling tricky situations with your boss.

- Building your senior network.

It's often said that people leave bosses, not companies, and that's something I've heard echoed by people who have done just that. I think it's also true that people will stay at an organisation because of their manager. Your relationship with your boss is not just important for you; it's important for your team. How you get on with your manager will impact on your performance at – and enjoyment of – your job and so will in turn impact on your team.

Your boss can be your advisor, ally and champion – or your blocker. You may have experienced one or both already in your career. I've experienced both and it made a huge impression on me, so let's look at how you can better manage this vital relationship so that it works really well for both of you. This isn't being 'political' or 'manipulative', or some other derogatory label, it's simply about being smart and applying intelligence to something, which, if taken for granted, can cost us dearly.

What if you have more than one boss? It's often the case: your 'line manager' may be a many-headed creature, comprising several different individuals. And there are usually other bosses, for example department head, Finance Director, Managing Director, CEO, with whom you come into contact on a regular basis, who have a direct impact on your career progress. To get clear on this I suggest a who's who.

Exercise: who's who round here?

Put your name in the middle circle below. Now think of the senior people you deal with, starting with your immediate manager(s). Next, add other senior managers and department heads, keeping those you work most closely with close to you in the map. If it helps, think of a recent project to make sure you've included everyone involved. By all means make a bigger version of this exercise if there's a large cast of characters.

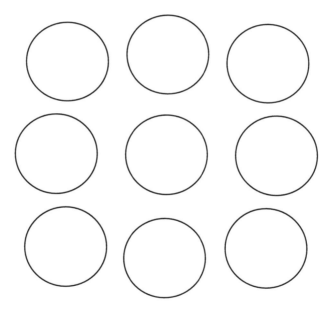

As you look at your who's who, note down words that come to mind about what each individual is like to deal with. What's their top priority? What do they value? Do they have a sense of urgency? Are they logical and systematic, or maybe a bit chaotic? Are they more of a 'people person'? Do they go on gut feel? Get four to five words down for each person. You might add a few things you know about them. How long have they worked here? Are they a huge Manchester United fan? Do they have shares in the company? Do they play in a band?

Now take a look at your map as a whole. What strikes you? You may have heaps of information about the characters you work with on a day-to-day basis. If you don't, what's the reason for that? What about the other cast members? Are there some you have a clear picture of, and others that are vague?

The main point of getting you to do this exercise it to increase your awareness of the relationships you have – or don't – with key players. Who are the people you spend most time with? Sometimes there may be people in the map you don't know or speak to at all. That might not be a bad thing. But if both you and they have been at the organisation a while, get curious about this lack of contact.

Many people find they're focusing very intensively on a few relationships that are vital to getting the work done. Understandable. However, it can benefit you to extend your network further. What happens if one or two of your close group leaves? What happens if one of the people in the outer limits of your map gets moved to a role that directly impacts yours? Building relationships with senior people isn't about being a creep: it's about survival. Identifying, mapping out and reflecting on your cast of characters is a sensible thing to do. We can overplay relationships that get cosy and comfortable, but actually have little impact on the overall work or our career. We can neglect crucial relationships and it might only become apparent when we really need them – too late. Here are some actions you may want to take with the people on your map, particularly those closest to you.

Find out what makes them tick

What do they want? What are their goals, and what results are they after? If they're going to be assessing you, how are they assessed? The simplest way to get answers to these important questions is to ask them. Pick the right time and place, but make sure you do it and take careful note of what they say. What do they see as important? Money? Promotion? Time with their family? Awards and recognition? A happy team? Being in the headlines? Some souls may be a bit reticent about this at first, and may perceive it as being somewhat intrusive, so tread gently and if necessary explain that you need to know so that you can work more effectively with them. This will take more than one conversation. Little and often is better than making a big deal of it. Working relationships – like any other kind – take time and trust to develop.

Find out what winds them up

This is equally important, as we can often make the mistake of thinking that we all get wound up by the same things. Not so. Again, ask them – and in this case, they probably won't hesitate to tell you. It could be lateness, (lack of) attention to detail, not being given the heads-up at the right time, long-winded communications, people who think out loud, long meetings, people who don't speak up, people who seem scattered and all over the place, poor productivity, too much information or not enough.

Put the time in

With your immediate manager(s) I recommend having regular 1:1 catch-up sessions. These might be daily, weekly or monthly – depending on the nature and intensity of your work. If it's high-volume, high-risk, high-budget, your 1:1s will need to be more frequent than if your work is more seasonal, or fluctuates, or is a steady trickle rather than a torrent.

Give the top line

In your 1:1 discussions, be brief and clear what the top line is. It can help to think of this as a headline. What's changed? What's working well? What do you need input on? Aim to generate options, solutions and actions, not more problems for your boss to deal with. Above all, arrive at these discussions prepared. Be on top of your numbers, dates and details, and be ready to answer several questions.

Deliver what you say you will, when you say you will. If you can't deliver (for whatever reason), give the heads up sooner rather than later, with what you're doing about it and the implications.

Q&A. What do I do if my boss...

Takes credit for my work?

In the old days of rigid hierarchies there was a greater risk (and acceptance) of this happening than nowadays. But it's still something to watch out for. If this is happening to you, you need to build a network of allies who know what's going on. It's no use bleating about someone else taking the credit for your work if you're the only person who knows it. Copy people in on emails and do them the courtesy of asking if they want to continue to be copied in. Ensure you're at key meetings so that you can comment and contribute. Be crystal clear about what you have done solo and what you have done with others by using 'I' and 'we' as appropriate.

Is a bully?

This can be complicated, yet it's essential you deal with it. Give in, and they get away with it. Skulk off to another team, department or employer, and chances are you'll encounter a similar character there too, so learn to deal with them.

Sometimes this person may just be loud and overbearing. In which case you will need to give them some feedback, remembering all the guidelines we explored earlier. Be completely clear and specific about what they say and do that you find problematic, the effect it has and what you would prefer they said or did. Brace yourself for a gruff response and the need to have this conversation a few times. Ultimately this kind of boss may have more invested in things (and themselves) staying the same rather than changing, so be patient.

If the behaviour is more extreme than that, be aware that it may be fear in disguise. Bullies can have large yet very frail egos. Whatever you do, don't take them on in public as everyone will get covered in nastiness when the ego is punctured. Instead, take careful note of what they say and do, in detail. You may have grounds for a grievance, or you may be making a mountain of a molehill and being over-sensitive. Think carefully about what you say and do too – it may be a case of you being someone who can dish it out but not take it. When you're clear in your own mind that this behaviour needs to be dealt with, talk to HR and get their advice. They may be aware of the problem and able to speak to the individual, they may explain that this is the nature of how things get done round here so learn to handle it, or they may only be able to sympathise. But don't feel you have to put up with this on your own.

Emails me at all hours – and expects a reply?

You need to train this individual – which will mean holding your nerve. Expecting a reply to an email sent at 11pm isn't generally reasonable unless you're in the midst of a major crisis. Bear in mind that many senior people are in meetings all day long and spend their evenings catching up with everyone (and themselves), as it's the only time they have. So this doesn't necessarily mean they expect you to respond immediately. Reply first thing the next day (that's working day, not weekend) and you should be fine. If you find you're being kept awake fretting about the thing, then draft a reply – and save it, do not send it. Re-read, edit and send it first thing the next working day. If you're finding evening emails are a persistent problem, time-suck and intrusion, check your email settings so you can impose a curfew. If necessary, have a conversation with your boss about what you're doing and why. Yes, everyone's working longer and harder, but that doesn't mean unlimited access 24/7.

Build your senior network

A good working relationship with a good boss is vital. But if it's your only upward connection, you're vulnerable. They may leave, be transferred elsewhere or promoted and unable to take you with them.

One senior manager I knew of had made a career out of making the Managing Director look good. Now this M.D. wasn't a particularly pleasant character, and many people found them difficult and untrustworthy to deal with. Yet the manager was always singing the M.D.'s praises and wouldn't hear a word against them. Over time people began to mistrust the manager, who became increasingly isolated. When the M.D. left somewhat suddenly the manager soon found they, too, were looking for another job. The anticipated offer from the ex-M.D. never materialised.

Now let's turn our attention to some of the other people on your map. They might be those with whom you work less closely. Or they could be very senior individuals to whom you don't know what to say. I'm not suggesting you suddenly start glad-handing them, asking how their favourite team did at the weekend. That would be really strange, for them and for you. So what to do?

Strengthen links

Someone in your orbit knows this person – how? It may be their work brings them into contact with this character more, or they have a good relationship with someone in the same department. Ask your contact what this character's like to work with, what's really important to them, and what they're an expert in. If your contact asks 'why?' you can simply tell them you're curious. Leave it at that for a while. The opportunity to talk with the person will crop up sooner or later at a social gathering, a charity fundraiser or a town hall meeting. When the opportunity arises you can introduce yourself or ask someone to do it for you.

Ask for advice

Most senior people are more than happy to dispense advice in their own area of expertise. Think of what they know and how that might help you. Maybe they have a good understanding of your client's business sector, or a geographic market, or a particular discipline. They could be someone who understands financial markets and their impact on your business. Or they might be an expert on digital film-making, or sponsorship, or PR. Ask them about it, and say why you're interested – and you'd better be interested. Find out what the challenges and opportunities are in their area of expertise and how they're handling them.

Be ready to help

Networking of any kind is about give and take. It's very easy to spot a 'taker'; the person who's in it solely for what they can get, without giving anything back. So be ready to help your expanding network of senior people. You may be thinking, 'What can I possibly offer that they would find valuable?' You'd be surprised. They may want help putting together a playlist for their daughter's party, or a secret tutorial in social media. They may value a talk for their team about one of your recent projects. Don't worry about how you'll offer them this without grovelling; senior people usually have no hang-ups about asking for what they need.

Sharpen your commercial savvy

As you manage upwards, grow your commercial awareness. Build the big picture: the past, present, and as much as humanly possible, the future, for your industry and broader sector. Commercially-savvy people tap into knowledge through industry and sector bodies, relevant publications and blogs, and a mix of formal and informal networks. They know the big challenges facing their employer, and have ideas about where the opportunities are.

What are your employer's objectives? For the next five years? For this current year? Some organisations are brilliant at keeping their people informed of their goals and ambitions, and if you work for one such, you've no excuses for not knowing where they want to go. As much as you possibly can, get some numbers, some clear measures of what achieving those objectives means. For example, it may be turnover, profit, number of clients, number of awards, number of overseas offices, clients retained, or promotions from within (and reduced recruitment costs). When you have your 1:1s with your boss, ask how you can contribute.

Summary:
manage upwards to survive and thrive

1. Your relationship with your boss – your immediate line manager – can be the most important professional relationship you have. So it's worth putting in the time and effort to make that relationship work well.

2. Quickly find out your boss's preferences and adapt to them. Do they want to be constantly involved or hands-off? Do they hate email and prefer face-to-face chat?

3. There are other senior figures in your organisation with whom you should build relationships. This doesn't mean being a creep; it means having some idea of what matters to that person and having something worthwhile to say about it.

4. Find out what makes your senior people tick, what winds them up, what motivates them, and how they prefer to communicate. Ask advice and be ready to respond to a request for help.

5. Work with your boss and senior people to build your commercial savvy. Learn what drives and drains the business, and what the opportunities are.

Resources

www.hbr.org has blog posts and books available on the topic, which may be useful for those of you in larger, more hierarchical organisations.

The Managing Upwards Pocketbook by Patrick Forsyth is handy and practical.

CHAPTER 10

FACE UP TO CONFLICT AND DEAL WITH IT

Conflict at work can take many forms: an all-out confrontation, a heated disagreement, a sticking point in negotiation, a challenge to a suggestion or a mere difference of opinion. Conflict of some kind or another is a fact of working life, so here's what we'll cover to help you face up to and deal with it:

- Spotting the signs that conflict is positive – or negative.

- When to deal with conflict – and when not to.

- Behaviours that help and hinder in conflict.

Conflict at work is inevitable, and in some instances healthy. Indeed, some organisations have challenge and disruption built into their processes. If there were no challenges or disagreements, something would be very wrong. That tends to happen when people are playing along with a domineering boss, for the sake of peace and quiet rather than the prosperity of the organisation, or when everyone believes their own hype and thinks they can do no wrong.

So you get the idea that it's not always a bad thing, yet that's very often the preconception. If conflict is a fact of life, how to deal with it? The answer depends on whether that conflict is positive or negative.

Signs that conflict is positive:

- When there is debate and everyone's opinion is respected, yet a conclusion, if not unanimous agreement, needs to be reached. A board meeting would be a good example.

- When there is a challenge, as in someone questioning how a suggestion or proposal was arrived at, testing the thinking and assumptions underlying the idea. 'What's the thinking behind this?' 'What's the evidence?' 'How can we do this differently?' This often happens in presentations, when the questioner is trying to assimilate the new – and may have a valid point.

- When there are constructive suggestions that build on an idea, adding possibilities, which may or may not be what the proposer had in mind. Again, this can be a feature of presentations, around strategy, creative ideas, or implementation.

- When there needs to be a disruptive 'sanity check', to ensure the right points have been covered, the right actions agreed upon. 'Have we covered everything?' 'What's missing?' 'What haven't we thought of?' 'What are the implications?' This is really handy when preparing for an important meeting.

You might think this isn't really your idea of conflict. Yet all these situations have the potential to escalate into something more serious– and someone in these situations may well feel tested. It can get tricky at the time, yet the overall intention is for the best, and the experience is ultimately positive.

Signs that conflict is negative:

- When people get humiliated, which can happen if someone goes too far in their criticism of anther's ideas and it gets personal.

- When it breeds resentment, such as when someone feels they're being picked on and not given fair hearing.

- When it negatively impacts performance, for example when a domineering board director drives through a financially drastic decision.

- When it destroys trust, such as when someone verbally attacks another in front of colleagues, or backtracks on a prior agreement when under pressure.

The overall intention here is often to win, no matter what the cost to others, the team or the organisation. An individual puts their own survival or superiority over and above the common good. Someone is going to get hurt.

When to deal with it – and when not to

Do you always have to deal with every conflict, and if so, how do you decide? There are times when it's unnecessary, unwise and potentially unhealthy to deal with conflict situations. More often there are times when it's essential to deal with conflict.

When not to

- If it's genuinely not a big deal. For example; Jo has suggested something you think isn't a good idea, but on gentle questioning from you she seems to have covered all the bases. If it goes down in flames it's not the end of the world and you would like to give her some autonomy rather than nit-pick. And who knows, she might get somewhere with it. Not much is at risk and it's not worth upsetting her over it. Typically these are one-off situations. If you find you're giving in to Jo against your better judgement and on a regular basis, this could become a big deal.

- If you're outflanked and losing. The client has come up with one reason after another, backed up with numbers, facts and dire consequences, why your proposal won't work. Not only that, your boss is clearly up for negotiating a compromise here. You're outflanked and losing, so don't make matters worse by making a stand. It won't do you any good and it won't change anything.

- You can bank some brownie points for the future. This option only works if you're explicit about it and get agreement, as in 'OK, this time we'll go along with doing the presentation your way, but at the next meeting I'll lead the way. Can we agree on that?'

- There's a short-term and necessary gain. This may simply be a case of keeping the peace, particularly if other people are present, or buying time to regroup.

> I saw this brilliantly done when a known loose cannon strode into our team meeting and let rip into what we had agreed without his knowledge. The team leader stood up, apologised to the loose cannon and promised to catch up with him immediately afterwards. Peace was achieved, momentarily, and everyone breathed a sigh of relief when the attacker left the room. Whilst it might have been hugely entertaining to witness the team leader take on the loose cannon right there and then, toe to toe, there would have a been a loser and that wouldn't have benefitted anyone. A more private discussion did take place not long after, and it may have been 'animated' in parts but it stayed private, so honours even.

When to deal with it

- When it's a bigger issue. So this time Jo's presentation seems to you be way off the mark, this is the third time it's happened, and she's getting loudly insistent that she won't change a single thing. We have a pattern going on here and it's getting problematic.

- Equally, the conflict may be of the positive kind, and relate to a bigger issue, for example; when people in your team identify ways to improve a time-honoured process. They're complaining, but it's because they know things can be better.

- When there is a lot at stake. This might be team morale, when a bully is being tolerated for example, and you need to step in and stop the rot and resentment or your relationship with your team will be damaged. Or there may be a great deal of money at stake, which could have serious implications for your employer. Or a professional relationship with a client or supplier is getting increasingly rocky to the point of people and profits being hurt.

- Likewise, it may be a positive example where there is a major opportunity and lots of healthy debate about how best to approach it. Collaboration, rather than avoidance, will be the way to go.

- When it impacts the long-term. When not dealing with the conflict adversely affects the long-term future of people and business, it needs to be dealt with. I've seen this happen in firms when the staff engagement survey delivers dreadful results, which certain people have tried to bury under the cloak of; 'Well, times are tough', wilfully ignoring clear indicators that management style is a problem. Positively viewed at another employer, who might be finding it tough too, a similar survey will be taken as a signal that long-term change is needed and that senior managers will have to work together to identify what they're going to do. Only then will they be able to attract the best people who want to contribute to better times ahead.

Behaviours to beware of in conflict

When the going gets a bit challenging, let alone really tough, our hot button gets hit and we react in ways that can make matters worse. Most of us do this without being consciously aware of it. Many behaviours in conflict situations are hard-wired in from an early age. See a parent attempting to deal with a tantrum-throwing child and you'll get the idea (and the exact same behaviour can be witnessed when a waiter deals with a very difficult customer). Just to be clear, here are a few examples of behaviour that's likely to make a tense situation worse:

- Reading the riot act, loudly. This one's often accompanied by a head-teacher tone and matching body language. Hands on hips or wagging fingers signal that the rules have been violated and will be re-stated until there is compliance. The result can vary from resentment to rebellion.

- Throwing a tantrum (and objects). Some football managers are known for 'teacup throwing' at the half-time team talk, as the pent-up frustration of 45 minutes' worth of poor play is finally vented. It's questionable behaviour in a dressing room, let alone a meeting room. The result ranges from fear-fuelled (and therefore unsustainable) improvement to all-out confrontation.

- Taking it personally and responding personally. This leads to a blame game where no-one wins, and can deteriorate into a character assassination. Damaged relationships result.

- Refusing to budge. This is like the toddler refusing to go to bed, giving the parent no alternative but to pick them up and put them there. This behaviour can give the other party no alternative but to exert their authority. Or get authority involved.

- Saying 'Oh all right then'. Giving in to someone for the sake of a quiet life may be a smart strategy (see 'when not to deal with conflict' above). But if it's the habitual response, problems will build up over time. The victor may then keep taking advantage, and others may spot the opportunity to imitate them. Resentment can build, especially if a particular individual gets their way more than others.

Spotted any behaviours that you default to? You're not alone if you have: when we deliver Zoomly's 'How to handle conflict' workshop, people are often surprised at how they are unwittingly making matters worse. So let's look at what to do instead.

Behaviours that help in conflict

If acting like the headmaster or a spoilt child isn't the way to go, what is? The first step to being more resourceful in conflict situations is to become extremely aware of how you feel, what you think and how to respond. What effect does that have, on you and the other person? How well does your response deal with the situation? Keep building this awareness, and as you do you will break free from being a slave to your own default settings.

The next step is to really listen to what people are saying when the going gets tough. What's important to them? What's being ignored, disrespected, threatened or seen as unfair? I once worked with a client who threw creative work around. She didn't hate it; she was scared to take it to her boss.

Ask respectful questions and avoid asking 'Why?' Of course, you may need to find out the reason why, but please use other questions to get there. Think of who uses 'Why?' incessantly – small children. What happens to them? They get told 'because I said so'.

By raising your self-awareness and really listening to others you will be wiser, more compassionate and better able to handle conflict. By all means revert to your inner House Captain when you're organising a team night out. Or be unabashed and playfully offer wild and wonderful ideas at a brainstorming session. Just be sure to have this wise and compassionate version of yourself handy for when it's needed.

How to deal with conflict?

Here are some strategies that you can try. It's essential to go into this with self-respect and respect for the other person, otherwise you risk being manipulative, which will come back to bite you. Which strategy you choose depends on who's involved and the situation. You decide.

Hope it will go away

This might be an effective strategy if the conflict is of the 'no big deal' kind. However, if you find you're adopting this strategy on a fairly frequent basis you may be missing opportunities to resolve the issue and build stronger relationships. You may be unwittingly painting yourself in the 'victim corner', which can find an outlet in emotional blackmail and manipulation. Better to be open and honest.

Don't say: 'No really, it's nothing. Nothing, OK?'

Do say (with a sincere smile): 'Honestly, it's not a big deal. If it were, I'd say.'

Go head to head

This is not usually a good career move, particularly if others are telling you this tends to be your default setting. But if it's to defend your corner, or particularly if you have good reason to believe that one of your team is being badly treated, be prepared to do battle and show you won't stand for it. Warning! Not for public consumption! Remember the team leader and the loose cannon who had a subsequent private conversation? This doesn't have to be a shouting match; in fact it's best if it's not. So don't go in there reading the riot act or whining like a spoilt child. The delivery style should be assertive, calm and rational. The content should have absolutely no wriggle room whatsoever, backed up with evidence, facts and observations.

Don't say: 'HOW DARE YOU SPEAK TO ME LIKE THAT IN FRONT OF THE CLIENT!!! WHAT THE *%@± WERE YOU THINKING? I THOUGHT WE HAD A DEAL! WE'RE GOING TO HAVE THIS OUT RIGHT NOW!'

Do say (with unflinching eye contact): 'I felt so humiliated when you called me 'Jellywobble' in front of the client. I thought we had a deal after the away-day that the childhood nicknames would stay strictly in our group. I guess I could have mentioned your nickname, but at the time I thought better of it. What assurance can you give me that something like this won't happen again?'

Reach a compromise

Also known as a trade-off, this is when there's give and take on both sides, so that both feel OK about it. This works well if you're both pushed for time, but have enough invested in the relationship to want to keep things running smoothly between you. You need to be very well prepared for this, otherwise there's a risk that the other party could out-manoeuvre you. So think ahead: what do they need and want? What 'trades' are you prepared to make? What are your non-negotiables or deal-breakers? Beware taking a stand here: keep the conversation going by asking respectful questions and listening really well to the responses you get. Sum up at the end of the conversation to ensure you are both completely clear.

Don't say: 'Oh all right then, you get the boardroom whenever your client comes in and we can have it every third Tuesday.'

'Look, we need to know that you'll always offer us this level of discount. Do you agree?'

Do say: 'What minimum discount would you be prepared to offer if we made you our preferred supplier? What volume are we talking about here?'

Build a bigger and better solution together

If it's a big deal, with lots at stake and potential long-term impact, this can be a great way to go. However, it does take time and may not reach resolution in just one conversation. It's vital that everyone can agree a common goal. Both parties may need to adjourn to do some more digging, come up with ideas and then reconvene. Our not-so-sparkling staff survey may be a good case in point, say with department heads and the HR team. It could take a while just to reach the stage where all parties agree that something should and can be done. Then they'll have to go away and think of exactly how, meet again and discuss ideas. You get the idea: there might not be a quick fix, but it's worth the (shared) effort.

Don't say: 'You know what? I'm busy, and anyway I think HR are perfectly capable of coming up with some shiny new rulebook for us.'

Do say: 'Can we agree what we want to achieve here, with everyone's input? Only then can we all realistically scope out what needs to be done and how long it's going to take us.'

"Can I just ask...

...what can I do if there's conflict between two of my team members?"

This is a very common problem and chances are the two protagonists have no idea how corrosive this is for everyone around them. How you respond will depend on your role. For example, if you manage both people then you have the responsibility to help them resolve their differences. This is not just for their own good, but for the health of the team. First, get really clear on the behaviour of both individuals; who does and says what and the impact it has. Then when you're sure of the facts, get advice from someone more experienced. That might be your own manager, a department head, a peer in another department or HR. Discuss and decide what to do, then do it. It may be that you have to go head to head with each person separately if the behaviour is really causing problems. Ideally, work with both people to build a bigger and better solution together.

If you're on the same level as the people involved, resist the temptation to wade in as The Great Peacekeeper. They could both turn their attention to you, and not in a good way. Instead, notice the effect the conflict is having, and only if you think it's potentially damaging enough should you have a quiet word with your manager. It may be that what you see as a barrage of abuse the protagonists just see as banter, so tread carefully.

Exercise: conflict action plan

You can apply the relevant points in this chapter to building a more effective working relationship with someone.

Name of person I experience most conflict with at work

What I say and do

What I think and feel

What they say and do

What the outcome is

What I will do differently next time

Summary:
face up to conflict and deal with it

1. 'Conflict' can range from a difference of opinion to an all-out hostile confrontation. So it's inevitable we will encounter some kind of conflict at work.

2. Some conflicts are actually positive. They may be a challenge to old patterns of doing things, or a desire to deliver the best. Other conflicts can be negative. People get hurt, resentments can fester, morale decline. Negative conflicts can impact the bottom line: through lost talent, lost opportunity and lost business.

3. We have default behaviours in conflict situations, based on our early experience. Sometimes these defaults are helpful, sometimes not. Chances are that when we're in a challenging situation, we will need to moderate our behaviour rather than just defaulting to behaviour that may be unhelpful. So stay very aware of what's going on, both for you and the other party.

4. Develop your wisdom and compassion by seeking to understand what's important for people in conflict. Ask respectful questions and really listen to the replies. Aim to find a common goal or shared ground.

5. We need to wise up about the different options we have in conflict situations. We may be more assertive, or acquiesce, or aim for collaboration.

Resources

http://www.dalecarnegie.co.uk/events/guide_books/
The Dale Carnegie organisation's website has useful free resources you can download, including a useful *Internal Conflict Resolution Guidebook*.

www.businessballs.com explains different approaches to dealing with conflict.

PART III
HOW TO BE ZOOMLY
AT WORK

CHAPTER 11

YES, YOU WILL GET FOUND OUT – AND IT'S OK!

Hands up if, while you've been working through this book, a little voice kept interrupting your thoughts, saying something like; 'I'll get found out!' – anyone? Fear of 'getting found out' is more common than you think. This particular career fear even has its own name: 'imposter syndrome'. You can probably hear your own personal imposter syndrome kicking in when your confidence has a wobble and you start to think that you're really not the right person for the job you have, let alone a promotion. In fact (says the toxic soundtrack in your head), you really shouldn't have bothered getting out of bed this morning! You get the idea. We can be our own biggest obstacle to being Zoomly at work, so we'll cover two points to help get out of our own way:

- Imposter syndrome and what to do about it.
- What to do if you *do* screw up.

Imposter syndrome

Imposter syndrome can kick in at any time. You won't be the first this has happened to, and you won't be the last. Millions of people suffer from it at some point in their careers, including the very successful. Oscar winner Meryl Streep said; "I don't know how to act anyway, so why am I doing this?" There is some evidence that women are more likely to suffer imposter syndrome than are men, but don't fall into the trap of thinking men never get this – they do. It's just that for men it can show up differently.

The toxic soundtrack, or internal dialogue, can be heard when we start telling ourselves things like:

'They'll find out I'm a fraud.'

'I'll go blank.'

'My team won't respect me.'

'How on earth will I be able to do it [insert any requirement of the role here]?'

'My colleagues will see right through me.'

'I'll be OK if I can avoid presentations.'

'They'll ask questions I can't answer.'

'If I use Bob for all the XYZ stuff (insert anything you're not great at here], I can get away with it.'

'I'll get humiliated in front of clients.'

'Sooner or later, I'll get found out.'

Self-defence against Imposter syndrome

There are steps you can take to put solid defences in place against attacks of imposter syndrome, so if you've found yourself listening to the dreaded toxic soundtrack, help is right here. Basically, this process is about being your own judge and jury.

First, gather the evidence. If that sounds familiar, it is. You gathered evidence earlier in the first part of this book. I'm a big believer in evidence, otherwise we may end up simply dreaming – or having self-inflicted nightmares. Think of a task or requirement of your role that is likely to fire off the 'I'm a fraud' internal dialogue. When I worked in advertising agencies the monthly income forecast would have my toxic soundtrack playing on max volume. For you, it might be making presentations, or having a tricky ten-minute conversation with a team member, or like me it might be around the numbers.

Now identify the evidence for the prosecution. In other words, what facts support this notion that you're a fraud when it comes to this task? Note down as much evidence as you can uncover. For example:

'I've never done this before.'

'It's not one of my strengths.'

'Last time I tried this, I stuffed it up.'

Keep going...

OK, time for the defence to step up and present evidence. Note down as many support points as you can. For example:

'Yes, I haven't done this before – and nor had my peers when they first stepped up to this role.'

'I have lots of experience of doing elements of this task; this is simply the first time I'll be doing the whole thing.'

'There are people here who can teach me and want to help.'

'My boss has heaps of examples.'

'I'm a good learner and with practice I can master this task.'

'I have been able to start at the beginning and learn a multitude of skills step by step and therefore that's exactly what I can do here.'

Now identify actions that will silence the prosecution and add weight to the defence. For example:

'I will ask Nicky (your #2) to help with this; it's one of her major strong points.'

'I will book a short meeting with Steve (your company's in-house expert on this) and prepare questions for him.'

'I will ask my boss for examples.'

'I will ask a colleague to watch me rehearse my

presentation and give me some feedback.'

'I will book a mini-training session with IT.'

There's no shame in asking for help on something that is new or strange to you. The same goes for a task that you believe is one of your weak points; by asking for help you are showing your determination to improve and develop. So now you have a list of actions, you can put a date and time against each one, and put them in your calendar.

If you can't generate actions, it's 'case dismissed'! Seriously, if you cannot identify a single action to take to silence this particular internal critic, it either isn't sufficiently relevant to your role or so far beyond your control that it just needs to be filed under 'not now thanks, I have other priorities.'

Do this process of gathering evidence for/against the imposter syndrome for each of your 'I'm going to get found out' fears. Our fears are often our psyche trying to protect us, whether that's from failure or some imagined foolishness. Successful people also have those fears, but they find ways to bust through them and the process I'm giving you here will help you do just that.

"Can I just ask...

...how can I admit I've never got the hang of spelling /spreadsheets/ apostrophes/ percentages/ etc?"

First of all, well done for getting this far in your career despite your perceived shortcomings. You must have impressed the people who've hired you for some reason. What do you think it is? Basic defects such as maths and grammar can be dealt with. Because they're often quite long-standing, it takes a sustained series of small steps to overcome them. A combination of simple 'how to' guides (check out the resources section for suggestions), friendly advice and constant practice will help you leave them behind.

What if you *do* screw up?

Now and again, you are bound to stuff up a task or fluff a small element of a presentation. Not all the time please note, not if you have identified and taken actions, but now and again it's going to happen. A useful mantra here is 'there is no failure, only feedback', which means that if we stop, consider the lessons learned and apply them, then we're not totally failing but rather learning and growing. Watch a toddler learning to walk: when they fall over, do they sit down and say to themselves; 'Shove this walking for a lark, I'm just going to sit down for the rest of today'? No. They get up, walk a bit more, fall over some more, get up and keep trying.

If the 'there is no failure, only feedback' mantra brings out the cynic in you, then my advice is to weigh up the level of risk involved. You simply won't have enough time to be equally perfectionist about everything, so you need to allocate time and attention around priorities. If that presentation is high priority then take time to prepare your content and yourself, rehearsing until you have nailed it. If that report is medium priority get on with it, but don't sweat. And if the task is low priority, not only do I recommend you stop worrying, but ask yourself if you should stop doing it altogether (and refer back to the Delegation chapter in this book).

When it comes to handling screw-ups, think about the example you want to set for your team. Would you be satisfied if someone tried to cover up an error? Or would you prefer they gave you the heads up and offered some solutions?

- Don't try to cover it up! Sooner or (worse) later you will get found out. Having to own up to the error is one thing, but explaining your way out of the deception will tangle you in knots or sharpen your ability to lie – and you don't want either.

- 'Fess up, to the right people in the right way. Say you're sorry. And before you do that, consider how you will deliver what retailers call 'service recovery'. This is when a drop in service standards is treated as an opportunity to turn the customer around from angry to delighted (of course this is most effective when the normal service standard is superb, which we will all do well to remember!). Explain how the error came about and what you're going to do about it, and/or how you will prevent it recurring.

- If you need to discuss a screw-up with your boss, go prepared with a plan and ensure you have details of the impact of the error, whether it's on finances, timing or relationship. They would rather have a heads-up from you earlier than learn about the problem from someone else later.

- If the mistake affects your peers in other areas, say your part of a presentation to senior managers or fellow members of a pitch team for example, identify the most influential of these stakeholders, start with them and work steadily through the group. Be honest. Ask for and offer support and go the extra mile for them next time.

- If your own team are the ones most affected by the error – maybe you agreed a deadline with a client that they think is way too tight – take the heat. Don't take it out on your team or expect them to pull out all the stops to bail you out. It's down to you to be contrite – both with regard to your team and your client – and mend the fences. Tough in the short term, but much more sustainable with your key people over time.

Many of our role models, many high-profile leaders, have failed at some point (and if you're not convinced that's so, get hold of some biographies and read all about it). Richard Branson was considered hopeless at school, Stephen Spielberg was rejected by the same film school three times and J.K. Rowling had her Harry Potter books rejected countless times. They learned from their setbacks, screw-ups and knocks and used them as fuel to improve.

Summary:
yes, you will get found out – and it's OK!

1. Imposter syndrome is so commonplace it has its own name. You are not the first, nor will you the last person who has moments of self-doubt.

2. We all have an inner soundtrack, or internal dialogue. Sometimes it can be positive. Sometimes it can be negative, and if we allow it to continue unchallenged it becomes corrosive.

3. The good thing about our inner soundtrack is that we can change it. The vital first step is to notice what it's saying on a regular, daily basis.

4. Our fears are sometimes well founded, and in those cases the remedies are usually clear. Often, our fears stem from self-protection that goes way, way back, and is no longer realistic or relevant. Gathering and examining evidence is the way to sort them and find solutions.

5. Everyone screws something up at some point. It's how you handle it that really matters. You can allow mistakes to be career-limiting or

career-defining, depending on how you handle them. Your call.

Resources

www.businessinsider.com Just enter the term in the search box and you'll find several posts about 'Imposter syndrome'.

CHAPTER 12

NEXT STEPS

Now it's over to you. How will you be Zoomly at work?

Make a commitment to step up and do the job you have to the best of your ability. That way, you will be in pole position to make the next step you really want.

How will you apply what you have learned in this book? Be really specific about what you will do, where, when, and with whom. Here are a few reminders to prompt you.

1. Where do you want to be? Make a commitment to revisit the 'All about you' exercises in Part I. Keep your goals handy and check your progress.

2. Communicate for clarity. Write 'upside down' – main point first then reasons why. Be crystal clear on actions – what, whom and when. Speak up in meetings and take an active part.

3. Focus on the right things. Remember to integrate the three kinds of time: Deadline Time, Duration Time and Diary Time. Do a 'Ta Dah!' list of things you've achieved recently. Compile a 'NOT to do' list and identify what you will delegate.

4. Delegate to develop people. Prepare well, brief clearly and get a dialogue going. Coach, support and encourage to get the right people doing the right work.

5. Tell people how they're doing. Practise a balance of praising and building, weighted to praising. Be sincere and specific about the behaviour and its impact. Give the recipient the mic and end the conversation well.

6. Bring out the best in your team. Stay alert to the stage of development your team is at. If the team members change then it's back to the first stage. Have clear goals, roles and ground rules.

7. Manage upwards to survive and thrive. Get to know your boss and what's important to them. Build more working relationships and broaden your network. Grow your organisational antennae.

8. Face up to conflict; it's a fact of life. Be selective about when to deal with conflict and when it's wise to avoid it. Identify everyday opportunities to practise dealing with conflict to develop your skills.

9. Yes you will get found out – and it's OK! Listen to your internal dialogue and change the track if it's getting toxic. What would a wise friend say?

10. Check out the resources in this book.

Make a commitment

My suggestion is to focus on no more than three areas at a time. Therefore you might pay special attention to your time management, focusing on the right things and doing a 'Ta Dah!' list. You may work on how you communicate with colleagues and key stakeholders. And you can take steps to manage upwards more effectively.

So what are you going to commit to that will make you Zoomly at work? List your three next steps here:

What I'll do	When I'll do it

Make sure you put a date against each step. Set a reminder in your calendar for four weeks from now, to check back in with your commitments and note your progress.

Here are some suggestions to help you keep on track:

Share this book with a buddy and meet up for a coffee and progress check. Arrange to call each other at certain times to ensure you've done what you said you would do.

Teach someone else the lessons you have learned from this book, because when we can teach another person, we're both demonstrating and mastering the skills.

Follow Zoomly's LinkedIn page, and keep in touch with us about how you're getting on. Email me dawn@zoomly.co.uk if you have any questions – and to tell me your success stories.

GOOD LUCK!

RESOURCES

Here are all the resources mentioned throughout this book, in one handy place.

All the books listed are available on Amazon.

Chapter 1: How did you get to here?

If you have enjoyed the activities in this chapter, you may enjoy *Manage Yourself, Manage Your Life: Vital NLP techniques for personal well-being and professional success* by Ian McDermott and Ian Shircore. Whilst based on Neuro-Linguistic Programming (NLP), the exercises are very accessible to non-NLP-ers.

Chapter 2: Where are you now?

Skills and capability tests

http://www.bbc.co.uk/skillswise offers numeracy and literacy tests

www.mensa.org.uk 'The high IQ Society'. So you can probably guess the kind of test on offer (for a small fee).

https://nationalcareersservice.direct.gov.uk This is a great site for people of all ages and academic levels. To access the skills assessments, select the Career Tools tab then choose Skills Health Check Tools and select tests appropriate for your education level (it goes up to PhD, so there are some pretty stiff tests). There's a range of tools, including working with numbers, solving abstract problems and working with written information. Free access and downloadable reports.

http://www.shldirect.com/en is global talent assessment company CEB-SHL's test preparation site, offering free and paid-for practice tests.

Psychometric tools

www.bps.org.uk Home of the British Psychological Society. Head for the 'Psychology and the public' tab and then 'Information for the public' which includes resources such as 'What's in a psychometric test?' The excellent research digest blog is accessible to all.

http://www.psychometricinstitute.co.uk has free practice psychometric assessments and aptitude tests. They also sell online courses offering more in-depth practice and help for those about to take assessments.

http://www.teamtechnology.co.uk/ offers a free 'Mental Muscle Diagram Indicator™', based on Myers Briggs theory (behind the Myers Briggs Type Indicator® or MBTI). Detailed reports based on your MMDI are available for a small fee.

Strengths assessments

http://www.authentichappiness.sas.upenn.edu/ questionnaires.aspx This is the University of Pennsylvania's Positive Psychology Center site, which offers heaps of free questionnaires. Registration required. I recommend the VIA Signature Strengths questionnaire.

http://www.cappeu.com/Realise2.aspx CAPP is the Centre for Applied Positive Psychology and Realise2 is their strengths assessment and development tool, used by major organisations. Individuals can complete their own Realise2 questionnaire online and get a report for a small fee. Check out the resources section of the website for free downloads and book sample chapters. I also recommend CAPP's books.

www.gallupstrengthscenter.com Here you can take the popular Clifton Strengthsfinder for a small fee.

Chapter 3: Where do I want to be?

http://www.ethics.org/resource/definitions-values Not-for-profit organisation that offers a long list of values with definitions.

http://www.missionstatements.com/ has lots of examples, from organisational to personal, plus a tool for you to create your own mission statement 'in under an hour'.

If you want to take a closer look at your career path, you may want to get hold of *Career Anchors* by Edgar Schein. There's a self-assessment booklet and another volume deals with the results. I also recommend *How to get a job you'll love* by John Lees.

Chapter 4: Communicate for clarity

www.moo.com/postcards to create your own postcards.

Check out Sheryl Sandberg's *Lean in: Women, Work and the Will to Lead* book to find her thoughts on interruptions. There's also a video interview with Ms Sandberg on www.hbr.com

If you want to learn from respected writers, *The Economist Style Guide* is a good investment.

Nervous about your grammar? *Eats, Shoots and Leaves* by Lynne Truss will prove invaluable.

Chapter 5: Focus on the right things – and make the best use of your time

http://evernote.com/ lots of people swear by this as the best way to stay on top of meetings and multiple projects across all their devices.

You can also enter 'Timesheet' into a search engine and download one that you like the look of.

Chapter 6: Delegate to develop people

www.blogs.hbr.org heaps of posts and tips for delegation.

http://www.businessballs.com/delegation.htm also has tips and techniques, often in the site author's forthright style.

Chapter 7: Tell people how they're doing

http://www.positivityratio.com/ Dr. Barbara Fredrickson's site with more on the 'positivity ratio', an online test and of course the best-selling *Positivity* book

There are some hilarious 'how not to' examples on YouTube

Chapter 8: Bring out the best in your team

http://www.missionstatements.com/team_mission_statements.html has lots of household-name examples of team mission statements for a range of work disciplines.

There are heaps of books out there on teams and how to get the best from them. My recommendation is *Effective Teamwork* by Professor Michael West because it's solidly evidenced and very practical. Professor West's work with teams in operating theatres has lowered patient mortality rates.

Chapter 9: Manage upwards to survive and thrive

www.hbr.org has blog posts and books available on the topic, which may be useful for those of you in larger, more hierarchical organisations.

The Managing Upwards Pocketbook by Patrick Forsyth is handy and practical.

Chapter 10: Face up to conflict and deal with it

http://www.dalecarnegie.co.uk/events/guide_books/ The Dale Carnegie organisation's website has free resources you can download, including a useful *Internal Conflict Resolution* Guidebook.

www.businessballs.com explains different approaches.

Chapter 11: Yes, you will get found out – and it's OK!

www.businessinsider.com Just enter the term in the search box and you'll find several posts about 'Imposter syndrome'.

Thank You

Thanks are due to all the people who've participated in training workshops I've run over the years. You are great fun to be around, a constant challenge (in a good way) – and it's a privilege to work with you. Thanks to our brilliant clients who keep engaging Zoomly to help bring the best out in your people. My fellow trainers deserve a big 'Thanks' for your insights and feedback, as well as your preparedness to have a go when I decide it's time for something new. Thanks to Mindy Gibbins-Klein, a.k.a. 'the Book Midwife', for helping this particular baby enter the world. Thanks also to Kevin Duncan for wise words and suggesting the title. Thanks to my husband Chris for your patience and support. And to all the people who have come up to me at the end of a training workshop and asked me a question: thank you, and I hope that I have given you what you needed.

About the author

Dawn Sillett MCIPD BSc (Hons) specialises in bringing the best out of creative professionals. Over the past fifteen years, she has designed and delivered training and coaching programmes for thousands of board directors, copywriters, newly-promoted managers, creative technologists and graduate trainees. Dawn is Managing Director of Zoomly, which specialises in fast, focused and effective training and coaching. Her work has taken her to every continent, providing high-energy, practical learning in London, Brussels, New York, Beirut, Moscow and beyond. Clients include AMV BBDO, WPP and Random House as well as industry bodies such as The Institute of Practitioners in Advertising and D&AD. Dawn's early career in the advertising industry involved blue chip brands and took her from London to Singapore. Dawn has a BSc (Hons) in Psychology and is a Chartered Member of the CIPD. When she's not being Zoomly, Dawn enjoys following her scuba-mad husband into caves, coral canyons and the occasional shipwreck.